Potatoes

The Essential Recipe Handbook

Publisher's Note:
Raw or semi-cooked eggs should not be consumed by babies, toddlers, pregnant women,
the elderly or those suffering from recurring illness.

Recipe Note:
All eggs and vegetables are medium sized, unless otherwise stated.

Publisher and Creative Director: Nick Wells
Project Editor: Cat Emslie
Photographers: Paul Forrester, Colin Bowling and Stephen Brayne
Home Economists & Stylists: Jaqueline Bellefontaine,
Mandy Phipps, Vicki Smallwood, Penny Stephens and Ann Nicol
Art Director: Mike Spender
Layout Design: Dave Jones
Digital Design and Production: Chris Herbert
Proofreader: Dawn Laker

Special thanks to: Polly Prior

09 11 13 12 10

1 3 5 7 9 10 8 6 4 2

This edition first published 2009 by
STAR FIRE
Crabtree Hall, Crabtree Lane
Fulham, London SW6 6TY
United Kingdom

www.star-fire.co.uk

Star Fire is part of the Foundry Creative Media Co. Ltd

© 2009 this edition The Foundry Creative Media Co. Ltd

ISBN 978-1-84786-545-8

A CIP record for this book is available from the British Library upon request.

Printed in China

Potatoes

The Essential Recipe Handbook

General Editor: Gina Steer

STAR FIRE

Contents

Vegetables 174

Hygiene in the Kitchen

It is important to remember that many foods can carry some form of bacteria. In most cases, the worst it will lead to is a bout of food poisoning or gastroenteritis, although for certain people this can be serious. The risk can be reduced or eliminated, however, by good hygiene and proper cooking.

Do not buy food that is past its sell-by date and do not consume food that is past its use-by date. When buying food, use the eyes and nose. If the food looks tired, limp or a bad colour or it has a rank, acrid or simply bad smell, do not buy or eat it under any circumstances.

Dishcloths and tea towels must be washed and changed regularly. Ideally, use disposable cloths and replace on a daily basis. More durable cloths should be left to soak in bleach, then washed in the washing machine at a high temperature. Keep hands, utensils and food preparation surfaces clean and do not allow pets to climb on to work surfaces. Avoid handling food if suffering from an upset stomach as bacteria can be passed on through food preparation.

Buying

Avoid bulk buying where possible, especially fresh produce. Fresh foods lose their nutritional value rapidly, so buying a little at a time minimises loss of nutrients. Check that any packaging is intact and not damaged or pierced at all. Store fresh foods in the refrigerator as soon as possible.

When buying frozen foods, ensure that they are not heavily iced on the outside and that the contents feel completely frozen. Ensure that they have been stored in the cabinet at the correct storage level and the temperature is below -18°C/ -0.4°F. Pack in cool bags to transport home and place in the freezer as soon as possible after purchase.

Preparation

Take special care when preparing raw meat and fish. Separate chopping boards should be used for each, and the knife, board

and your hands should be thoroughly washed before handling or preparing any other food. Good quality plastic boards are available in various designs and colours. This makes differentiating easier and the plastic has the added hygienic advantage of being washable at high temperatures in the dishwasher. If using the board for fish, first wash in cold water, then in hot to prevent odour.

When cooking, be particularly careful to keep cooked and raw food separate to avoid any contamination. It is worth washing all fruits and vegetables regardless of whether they are going to be eaten raw or lightly cooked. This rule should apply even to prewashed herbs and salads.

Do not reheat food more than once. If using a microwave, always check that the food is piping hot all the way through – in theory, the food should reach 70°C/158°F and needs to be cooked at that temperature for at least three minutes to ensure that all bacteria are killed.

All poultry must be thoroughly thawed before using. Remove the food to be thawed from the freezer and place in a shallow dish to contain the juices. Leave the food in the refrigerator until it is completely thawed. A 1.4 kg/3 lb whole chicken will take about 26–30 hours to thaw. To speed up the process, immerse the chicken in cold water, making sure that the water is changed regularly. When the joints can move freely and no ice crystals remain in the cavity, the bird is completely thawed. Once thawed, remove the wrapper and pat dry. Place the chicken in a shallow dish, cover lightly and store as close to

the base of the refrigerator as possible. The chicken should be cooked as soon as possible.

Some foods can be cooked from frozen, including many prepacked foods such as soups, sauces, casseroles and breads. Where applicable, follow the manufacturers' instructions. Vegetables and fruits can also be cooked from frozen, but meats and fish should be thawed first. The only time food can be refrozen is when the food has been thoroughly thawed then cooked. Once the food has cooled, then it can be frozen again, but it should only be stored for one month.

All poultry and game (except for duck) must be cooked thoroughly. When cooked, the juices will run clear on the thickest part of the bird – the best area to try is usually the thigh. Other meats, like beef, lamb and pork, should be cooked right the way through. Fish should turn opaque, be firm in texture and break easily into large flakes.

Make sure leftovers are reheated until piping hot and that any sauce or soup reaches boiling point first.

Storing, Refrigerating and Freezing

Meat, poultry, fish, seafood and dairy products should all be refrigerated. The temperature of the refrigerator should be between 1–5°C/34–41°F, while the freezer temperature should not rise above -18°C/-0.4°F. To ensure the optimum temperature, avoid leaving the door open for long periods. Try not to overstock as this reduces the airflow inside and therefore the effectiveness in cooling the food within.

When refrigerating cooked food, allow it to cool down quickly and completely before refrigerating. Hot food will raise the temperature of the refrigerator and possibly affect or spoil other food stored in it.

Food should always be covered. Raw and cooked food should be stored in separate parts of the refrigerator. Cooked food should be kept on the top shelves, while raw meat, poultry and fish should be placed on the bottom to avoid drips and cross-contamination. It is recommended that eggs be refrigerated in order to maintain their freshness and shelf life.

Regularly clean, defrost and clear out the refrigerator and freezer – it is worth checking the packaging to see exactly how long each product is safe to freeze. Take care that frozen foods are not stored in the freezer for too long. Blanched vegetables can be stored for one month; beef, lamb, poultry and pork for six months; and unblanched vegetables and fruits in syrup for a year. Oily fish and sausages should only be stored for three months. Dairy products can last four to six months, while cakes and pastries can be kept in the freezer for three to six months.

High-risk Foods

Certain foods may carry risks to people who are considered vulnerable, such as the elderly, the ill, pregnant women, babies, young infants and those suffering from a recurring illness.

There is a slight chance that some eggs carry the bacteria salmonella. Cook the eggs until both the yolk and the white are firm to eliminate this risk. Pay particular attention to dishes and products incorporating lightly cooked or raw eggs, such as hollandaise sauce, mayonnaise, mousses, soufflés, meringues, custard-based dishes, ice creams and sorbets. Certain meats and poultry also carry the potential risk of salmonella and so should be cooked thoroughly until the juices run clear and there is no pinkness left. Unpasteurised products such as milk, cheese (especially soft cheese), pâté and meat (raw and cooked) all have the potential risk of listeria and should be avoided.

When buying seafood, buy from a reputable source which has a high turnover to ensure freshness. Fish should have bright, clear eyes, shiny skin and bright pink or red gills. The fish should feel stiff to the touch, with a slight smell of sea air and iodine. The flesh of fish steaks and fillets should be translucent with no signs of discolouration. Molluscs such as scallops and mussels are sold fresh and are still alive. Avoid any that are open or do not close when tapped lightly; also discard any that do not open after cooking. In the same way, univalves such as cockles or winkles should withdraw back into their shells when lightly prodded. When choosing cephalopods, such as squid and octopus, they should have a firm flesh and pleasant sea smell.

As with all fish, whether it is shellfish or sea fish, care is required when freezing it. It is imperative to check whether the fish has been frozen before. If it has been frozen, then it should not be frozen again under any circumstances.

Nutrition: The Role of Essential Nutrients

A healthy and well-balanced diet is the body's primary energy source. In children, it constitutes the building blocks for future health as well as providing lots of energy. In adults, it encourages self-healing and regeneration within the body. A well-balanced diet will provide the body with all the essential nutrients it needs. This can be achieved by eating a variety of foods, demonstrated in the pyramid below.

FATS

PROTEINS
milk, yogurt   meat, fish, poultry,
and cheese   eggs, nuts and pulses

**FRUITS AND
VEGETABLES**

STARCHY CARBOHYDRATES
cereals, potatoes, bread, rice and pasta

FATS

Fats fall into two categories: saturated and unsaturated. Fats are an essential part of the diet as they are a source of energy and provide essential fatty acids and fat-soluble vitamins, but it is very important that a healthy balance is achieved. The right balance should boost the body's immunity to infection and keep muscles, nerves and arteries in good condition. Saturated fats are of animal origin and can be found in dairy produce, meat, eggs, margarines and hard white cooking fat (lard) as well as in manufactured products such as pies, biscuits and cakes. A high intake of saturated fat over many years has been proven to increase heart disease and blood cholesterol levels and often leads to weight gain. Lowering the amount of saturated fat that we consume is very important, but this does not mean that it is good to consume lots of other types of fat.

There are two kinds of unsaturated fats: polyunsaturated and monounsaturated. Polyunsaturated fats include safflower, soya bean, corn and sesame oils. The Omega-3 oils in polyunsaturated fats have been found to be beneficial to coronary health and can encourage brain growth and development. They are derived from oily fish such as salmon, mackerel, herring, pilchards and sardines. It is recommended that we should eat these types of fish at least once a week. Alternative liver oil supplements are also available. The most popular oils that are high in monounsaturates are olive oil, sunflower oil and peanut oil. Monounsaturated fats are also known to help reduce levels of cholesterol.

PROTEINS

Composed of amino acids – proteins' building blocks – proteins perform a wide variety of essential functions for the body, including supplying energy and building and repairing tissues. Good sources of proteins are eggs, milk, yogurt, cheese, meat, fish, poultry, nuts and pulses. (See the second level of the pyramid.) Some of these foods, however, contain saturated fats. To strike a nutritional balance, eat generous amounts of vegetable protein foods such as soya, beans, lentils, peas and nuts.

MINERALS

CALCIUM Important for healthy bones and teeth, nerve transmission, muscle contraction, blood clotting and hormone function. Also promotes a healthy heart and skin, relieves aching muscles and bones, maintains the correct acid–alkaline balance and reduces menstrual cramps. Good sources are dairy products, small bones of small fish, nuts, pulses, fortified white flours, breads and green leafy vegetables.

CHROMIUM Balances blood sugar levels, helps to reduce cravings, improves lifespan, helps protect DNA and is essential for heart function. Good sources are brewer's yeast, wholemeal bread, rye bread, oysters, potatoes, green peppers, butter and parsnips.

IODINE Important for the manufacture of thyroid hormones and for normal development. Good sources are seafood, seaweed, milk and dairy.

IRON As a component of haemoglobin, iron carries oxygen around the body. It is vital for normal growth and development. Good sources are liver, corned beef, red meat, fortified breakfast cereals, pulses, green leafy vegetables, egg yolk, cocoa and cocoa products.

MAGNESIUM Important for efficient functioning of metabolic enzymes and development of the skeleton. Magnesium promotes healthy muscles by helping them to relax and is therefore good for PMS. It is also important for heart muscles and the nervous system. Good sources are nuts, green vegetables, meat, cereals, milk and yogurt.

PHOSPHORUS Forms and maintains bones and teeth, builds muscle tissue, helps maintain pH of the body and aids metabolism and energy production. Phosphorus is present in almost all foods.

POTASSIUM Enables processing of nutrients; promotes healthy nerves and muscles; maintains fluid balance; helps secretion of insulin for blood sugar control; relaxes muscles; maintains heart functioning and stimulates gut movement. Good sources are fruit, vegetables, milk and bread.

SELENIUM Antioxidant properties help to protect against free radicals and carcinogens. Selenium reduces inflammation, stimulates the immune system, promotes a healthy heart and helps vitamin E's action. Necessary for the male reproductive system and for metabolism. Good sources are tuna, liver, kidney, meat, eggs, cereals, nuts and dairy products.

SODIUM Important in helping to control body fluid, preventing dehydration. Sodium is involved in muscle and nerve function and helps move nutrients into cells. All foods are good sources. Processed, pickled and salted foods are richest in sodium but should be eaten in moderation.

ZINC Important for metabolism and healing; aids ability to cope with stress; promotes a healthy nervous system and brain, especially in the growing foetus; aids bone and tooth formation and is essential for energy. Good sources are liver, meat, pulses, whole-grain cereals, nuts and oysters.

VITAMINS

BIOTIN Important for metabolism of fatty acids. Good sources of biotin are liver, kidney, eggs and nuts.

FOLIC ACID Critical during pregnancy for the development of the brain and nerves. It is always essential for brain and nerve function and is needed for utilising protein and red blood cell formation. Good sources are whole-grain cereals, fortified cereals, green leafy vegetables, oranges and liver.

VITAMIN A Important for cell growth and development and for the formation of visual pigments in the eye. Vitamin A comes in two forms: retinol and beta-carotene. Retinol is found in liver, meat and whole milk. Beta-carotene is a powerful antioxidant and is found in red and yellow fruits and vegetables such as carrots, mangoes and apricots.

VITAMIN B1 Important in releasing energy from carbohydrate-containing foods. Good sources are yeast and yeast products, bread, fortified breakfast cereals and potatoes.

VITAMIN B2 Important for metabolism of proteins, fats and carbohydrates to produce energy. Good sources are meat, yeast extracts, fortified breakfast cereals and milk and its products.

VITAMIN B3 Required for the metabolism of food into energy. Good sources are milk, fortified cereals, pulses, meat, poultry and eggs.

VITAMIN B5 Important for the metabolism of food and energy production. All foods are good sources but especially fortified breakfast cereals, whole-grain bread and dairy products.

VITAMIN B6 Important for metabolism of protein and fat. Vitamin B6 may also be involved in the regulation of sex hormones. Good sources are liver, fish, pork, soya beans and peanuts.

VITAMIN B12 Important for the production of red blood cells and DNA. It is vital for growth and the nervous system. Good sources are meat, fish, eggs, poultry and milk.

VITAMIN C Important for healing wounds and the formation of collagen, which keeps skin and bones strong. It is an important antioxidant. Good sources are fruits, especially soft summer fruits, and vegetables.

VITAMIN D Important for absorption and handling of calcium to help build bone strength. Good sources are oily fish, eggs, whole milk and milk products, margarine and, of course, sufficient exposure to sunlight, as vitamin D is made in the skin.

VITAMIN E Important as an antioxidant vitamin helping to protect cell membranes from damage. Good sources are vegetable oils, margarines, seeds, nuts and green vegetables.

VITAMIN K Important for controlling blood clotting. Good sources are cauliflower, Brussels sprouts, lettuce, cabbage, beans, broccoli, peas, asparagus, potatoes, corn oil, tomatoes and milk.

CARBOHYDRATES

Carbohydrates are an energy source and come in two forms: starch and sugar. Starch carbohydrates are also known as complex carbohydrates and they include all cereals, potatoes, breads, rice and pasta. Eating whole-grain varieties of these foods also provides fibre. Diets high in fibre are believed to be beneficial in helping to prevent bowel cancer and keep cholesterol down. Sugar carbohydrates – also known as fast-release because they provide a quick fix of energy – include sugar and sugar-sweetened products. Other sugars are lactose (from milk) and fructose (from fruit).

Varieties of Potatoes and Storage

The humble potato is generally taken for granted and the versatility and huge number of varieties of this delicious vegetable are often forgotten. Worldwide, there are thousands of different types of potatoes and for about two-thirds of the world, they are the staple food. In this country, almost three-quarters of main crop potatoes are made up of just five varieties. Consumers, however, have gradually become more demanding so a wider range of potatoes suitable for different uses is now available. Although you will still find bags simply labelled 'red' and 'white' in super-markets, alongside them is also a selection of named varieties. Many of the old varieties of potato are currently being revived, as well as new ones being created.

Potatoes are classified according to how early in the season they are ready for harvesting and are named as follows: first early, second early and main crop. The first earlies are the first new potatoes on the market; they are very fresh and young and the skins can simply be rubbed off. The second earlies are still new potatoes, but their skins will have begun to set. These potatoes will be difficult to scrape and are better cooked in their skins. Main crop potatoes are available all year round and may have been stored for several months. Individual potato varieties have their own characteristics. Some main crop varieties are better for boiling than baking and vice versa, so choose the most appropriate type of potato for the dish being prepared. Check the label, ask your retailer or refer to the list below for guidance.

Ailsa (main crop) These medium-sized potatoes are round or oval with white skins and creamy-coloured, floury flesh. Ailsa potatoes are excellent for boiling and chipping.

Anya (second early) These speciality, knobbly, oval-shaped potatoes have a pinkish skin and white flesh. They have a nutty flavour and waxy texture and are at their best when boiled or used in salads.

Arran Comet (first early) These round, and sometimes oval, new potatoes have a white skin and creamy flesh. Large ones are good for chipping.

Arran Pilot (first early) The firm flesh of these potatoes makes them an ideal choice for salads. They have white flesh and skins.

Arran Victory (main crop) These oval-shaped potatoes have a deep purple skin and a bright white flesh. They are the oldest variety of Arran potatoes still available. Arran Victory potatoes have a very floury texture and flavour and are excellent for baking and boiling. Currently, they are undergoing a revival – it is well worth seeking this variety out.

Asperge (second early) Also known as 'la ratte' and 'cornichon', these potatoes have a yellow skin and a creamy, very waxy flesh. They are good steamed or boiled and are perfect for salads.

Belle de Fontenay (early main crop) These long potatoes often have a curved shape. Their skins are pale yellow and their flesh is firm, waxy and yellow. They have a wonderful buttery flavour and are particularly good boiled, in salads or mashed.

Bintje (main crop) With a pale yellow skin and flesh, these potatoes are suitable for all cooking methods and make particularly good chips.

Cara (late main crop) These potatoes may be white or red, round or oval. The flesh is creamy-coloured with a mild flavour and waxy texture. Cara are good all-round potatoes.

Catriona (second early) Kidney-shaped potatoes with purple markings around the eyes on the skin and a pale yellow flesh. They have a delicious flavour and are ideal for baking, boiling and mashing.

Charlotte (main crop) Oval or pear-shaped potatoes with pale yellow skin and flesh, a firm, waxy texture and a flavour not unlike chestnuts. They are particulary good boiled, steamed and in salads but can also be baked.

Cleopatra (first early) These oval new potatoes are suitable for boiling, have pink or red skin and a light-yellow, dense flesh.

Colmo (first early) Medium round or oval, these potatoes have a white skin and firm golden flesh. Their texture and colour make them particularly good for mashing.

Desiree (main crop) Probably the world's most popular red-skinned potatoes with pale yellow flesh, a firm texture and good flavour. These potatoes are good all-rounders and are great for both mashing and roasting. They also hold their shape well enough for boiling.

Diamont (main crop) These potatoes were a common and popular variety in the 1930s and are still available now. They are long and oval shaped with a rough, white skin and a firm, waxy yellow interior. Their flavour is slightly sharp and nutty.

Duke of York (first early) These long, oval new potatoes have a sweet flavour, firm texture, pale creamy skins and light yellow flesh. A red-skinned variety is also available.

Epicure (first early) Round potatoes with white, or sometimes pink-tinged, skin, creamy, firm flesh and a distinctive flavour. Suitable for both boiling and baking.

Estima (second early) Oval-shaped potatoes with a light yellow skin and flesh. Their firm, moist texture and subtle flavour make them good baking potatoes. These potatoes were the first yellow-fleshed potatoes to become popular.

Golden Wonder (late main crop) These large, oval potatoes have a dark, russet-coloured skin and light yellow flesh. They are excellent for baking and their floury texture makes them especially good for crisps.

Home Guard (first early) Round or slightly oval, with white skins and creamy-coloured flesh, these potatoes have a dry, floury texture and a good flavour with slightly bitter overtones. These potatoes are ideal for boiling, roasting and chipping. They were a favourite during the Second World War and are one of the first varieties of new potatoes available.

Jersey Royals (second early) The best and most popular new potatoes, Jersey Royals have a creamy-coloured skin and flesh and can be served either hot or cold. When cooked (boiled or steamed), they are tender rather than firm and are best served whole, with or without the skins.

Kerr's Pink (late main crop) Round, pink-skinned potatoes with creamy-white flesh and a floury texture, these potatoes are suitable for boiling, baking, mashing, roasting and chipping.

King Edward (main crop) These large, white-skinned potatoes are among the best known and most popular. They

have creamy-coloured, very floury flesh and are good all-rounders. They are particularly suited to roasting and baking, but are not so good for salads.

Marfona (second early) These are good baking potatoes, also suitable for boiling, but not for roasting.

Maris Bard (first early) These white-skinned potatoes have firm, waxy flesh with a slightly earthy taste. They are good for boiling and suitable for most other methods. They should be avoided, however, late in the season when they lose their flavour and are in danger of disintegrating during cooking.

Maris Peer (second early) These potatoes have white flesh and skins, with an excellent flavour. They are good for salads as well as boiling and steaming.

Maris Piper (main crop) This is one of the best known and popular potato varieties on sale. It has a creamy coloured flesh and a white-to-yellow skin – although it is regarded as a 'white' potato. It is widely available and can be baked, fried, boiled, roasted and mashed.

Morag (main crop) These potatoes have a pale skin and a white, waxy flesh. Serve them boiled, steamed or baked.

Nadine (second early) These potatoes are available in two sizes. There are the small new potatoes and the slightly larger-sized potatoes which are suitable for baking. Nadine potatoes have creamy-yellow skins and white, waxy flesh, but their flavour is somewhat bland.

Pentland Javelin (first early) These new potatoes have very white, smooth skins and milky-white flesh. These potatoes are ideal for salads, but are also good boiled or steamed.

Pentland Squire (main crop) Usually white skinned, but occasionally russet, the flesh of these potatoes is very white. Their floury texture makes them perfect for baking. They are also good for boiling and mashing, but are poor in salads.

Pink Fir Apple (main crop) These knobbly, misshapen potatoes have white skins with a pinkish blush and a pale yellow flesh. They are firm and waxy with a delicious nutty flavour and have many of the characteristics of new potatoes. They are best cooked in their skins as their shape makes them extremely difficult to peel and are good steamed, boiled and served cold in salads.

Shelagh (main crop) This Scottish variety has a creamy flesh and pinkish patches all over the skin. The waxy texture of these potatoes makes them good for boiling, steaming or chipping.

Wilja (second early) These potatoes have pale yellow skins and flesh. They are good, flavoursome all-rounders and hold their shape when cooked, so are particularly suitable for salads, boiling and steaming. They can also be used for baking and roasting.

Sweet Potatoes These potatoes are imported from tropical areas of the Americas and from many other hot countries around the world. Their skins are red and the flesh inside is either white or orange. Orange-fleshed sweet potatoes have a denser, waxier texture and tend to hold their shape better, whereas white-fleshed ones are starchier and not quite as sugary. It is impossible to tell from the outside what colour the flesh will be within, so unless labelled you may need to scrape off a small patch of skin. Treat in much the same way as ordinary potatoes – bake, mash or fry.

Buying and Storage

When buying potatoes, always choose ones with smooth, firm skins. When purchasing new potatoes, check that they are really young and fresh by scraping the skin – it should peel away very easily. Only buy the quantity you need and use within a couple of days. Check main crop potatoes to make sure that they are firm and not sprouting or showing any signs of mould. Avoid buying and discard any potatoes with greenish patches or carefully cut them out. These parts of the potato are toxic and a sign that they have been stored in light.

Potatoes should be stored in a cool, dark place but not in the refrigerator as the dampness will make them sweat, causing mould to grow. If the potatoes come in plastic bags, take them out and store in a paper bag or on a vegetable rack. If you prefer to buy in bulk, keep the potatoes in a cold, dark, dry place such as a larder or garage, making sure that they do not freeze in cold weather.

Sweet potatoes should be stored in a cool, dry place but, unlike ordinary potatoes, do not need to be kept in the dark.

Cooking Techniques for Potatoes

Generally, new potato varieties have a firm and waxy texture that do not break up during cooking, so are ideal for boiling, steaming and salads. Main crop potatoes, on the other hand, have a more floury texture and lend themselves to mashing and roasting – both types are suitable for chips. When cooking potatoes, it is important to make sure the potatoes that you are using are the correct type for the dish being prepared. Whichever way you choose to serve potatoes, allow 175–225 g/6–8 oz per person.

Boiling Potatoes

New Potatoes

Most of the new potatoes available nowadays are fairly clean – especially those sold in supermarkets – and simply need a light scrub before cooking in their skins. If the potatoes are very dirty, use a small scrubbing brush or scourer to remove both the skins and dirt. Add them to a pan of cold, salted water and bring to the boil. Cover the pan with a lid and simmer for 12–15 minutes or until tender. Add a couple of sprigs of fresh herbs to the pan if you like – fresh mint is traditionally used to flavour potatoes. Drain the potatoes thoroughly and serve hot, tossed in a little melted butter or, for a change, a tablespoon of pesto. The skins of first early new potatoes will peel away easily, but second earlies should be served in their skins or peeled when cooked (hold the hot potatoes with a fork to make this easier). Very firm new potatoes can be added to boiling water, simmered for 8 minutes, then left to stand in the hot water for a further 10 minutes until cooked through.

'Old' (Main Crop) Potatoes

Choose a main crop potato suitable for boiling, then thinly peel and cut into even-sized pieces. Add to a saucepan of cold, salted water and bring to the boil. Cover the pan with a lid and simmer for 20 minutes, or until tender.

Alternatively, you can cook the potatoes in their skins and peel them after cooking. (It is particularly important to cook floury potatoes gently or the outsides may start to fall apart before they are tender in the centre. Drain the potatoes in a colander, then return them to the pan to dry out over a very low heat for 1–2 minutes.) If you are planning to serve the potatoes mashed, roughly mash them and add a knob of butter and 2 tablespoons of milk per person. Mash until smooth, either with a hand masher, mouli grater or a potato ricer. Season to taste with salt, freshly ground black pepper and a little freshly grated nutmeg if liked, then beat for a few seconds with a wooden spoon until fluffy. As an alternative to butter, use a good-quality olive oil or crème fraîche. Finely chopped red and green chillies, crispy-cooked crumbled bacon, fresh herbs or grated Parmesan cheese can also be stirred in for additional flavour.

Steaming Potatoes

All potatoes are suitable for steaming. Floury potatoes, however, are ideal for this method of cooking as they fall apart easily.

New and small potatoes can be steamed whole, but larger ones should be cut into even-sized pieces. Place the potatoes in a steamer, colander or sieve over boiling water and cover. Steam for 10 minutes if the potatoes are very small or, if they are cut into large chunks, cook for 20–25 minutes.

Frying Potatoes

Chipped Potatoes

To make chipped potatoes (commonly known as chips), wash, peel and cut the potatoes into 1.5 cm/⅝ inch slices. Cut the slices into long strips about 1.5 cm/⅝ inches wide. Place the strips in a bowl of cold water and leave for 20 minutes, then drain and dry well on kitchen paper – moisture will make the fat spit. Pour some oil into a deep, heavy-based saucepan or deep-fat fryer, making sure that the oil does not go any further than halfway up the sides of the pan. Heat the oil to 190°C/375°F, or until a chip dropped into the fat rises to the surface straight away and is surrounded by bubbles. Put the chips into a wire basket and lower into the oil and cook for 7–8 minutes, or until golden. Remove and increase the heat of the oil to 200°C/400°F. Lower the chips into the oil again and cook for 2–3 minutes, or until they are crisp and golden brown. Drain on kitchen paper before serving.

Slightly finer chips are known as pommes frites, even finer ones as pommes allumettes and the finest of all as pommes pailles (straw chips). Paper-thin slices of peeled potatoes, cut with a sharp knife or using a mandoline or food processor, can be deep-fried a few at a time to make crisps or game chips.

Healthy Chips

To make lower-fat chips, preheat the oven to 200°C/400°F/Gas Mark 6 and place a nonstick baking tray in the oven to heat up. Cut the potatoes into chips as above or into chunky wedges, if preferred. Put the chips or wedges in a pan of cold water and quickly bring to the boil. Simmer for 2 minutes, then drain in a colander. Leave for a few minutes to dry, then drizzle over 1½–2 tablespoons of olive or sunflower oil and toss to coat. Tip on to the heated baking tray and cook in the preheated oven for 20–25 minutes, turning occasionally until golden brown and crisp.

Sautéed Potatoes

Cut peeled potatoes into rounds about 0.5 cm/¼ inch thick and pat dry. Heat 25 g/1 oz unsalted butter and 2 tablespoons of oil in a large, heavy-based frying pan until hot. Add the potatoes in a single layer and cook for 4–5 minutes until the undersides are golden. Turn with a large fish slice and cook the other side until golden and tender. Drain on kitchen paper and sprinkle with a little salt before serving.

Baking Potatoes

Allow a 300–350 g/11–12 oz potato per person and choose a variety such as Maris Piper, Cara or King Edward. Wash and dry the potatoes, prick the skins lightly, then rub each one with a little oil and sprinkle with salt. Bake at 200°C/400°F/Gas Mark 6 for 1–1½ hours, or until the skins are crisp and the centres are very soft. To speed up the cooking time, thread on to metal skewers as this conducts heat to the middle of the potatoes.

Roasting Potatoes

For crisp and brown outsides and fluffy centres, choose potatoes suitable for baking. Thinly peel the potatoes and cut into even-sized pieces. Drop them into a pan of boiling, salted water and simmer for 5 minutes. Turn off the heat and leave for a further 3–4 minutes. Drain well and return the potatoes to the pan over a low heat for a minute to dry them and to roughen the edges. Carefully transfer them to a roasting tin containing hot oil or dripping. Baste well, then bake at 220°C/425°F/Gas Mark 7 for 20 minutes. Turn them and cook for a further 20–30 minutes, turning and basting at least one more time. Serve as soon as the potatoes are ready.

Potato Croquettes

Mash dry, boiled potatoes with just a little butter or olive oil, then stir in 1 egg yolk mixed with 1–2 tablespoons of milk or crème fraîche to make a firm mixture. Shape the mashed potatoes into small cylinders about 5 cm/2 inches long, rolling them in flour. Dip in beaten egg and then in fresh, white breadcrumbs. Chill the croquettes in the refrigerator for 30 minutes. Place a little unsalted butter and oil in a heavy-based frying pan and slowly heat until the butter has melted. Shallow fry the croquettes, turning occasionally until they are golden brown and crisp.

Rosti

Parboil peeled, waxy potatoes in boiling, salted water for 8 minutes, drain and leave to cool before coarsely grating into a bowl. Season well with salt and freshly ground black pepper and freshly chopped herbs if liked. Heat a mixture of unsalted butter and oil in a heavy-based frying pan until bubbling. Add tablespoonfuls of the grated potato into the pan and flatten with the back of a fish slice. Cook over a medium heat for about 7 minutes, or until crisp and golden. Turn and cook the other side.

Cooking Potatoes in a Clay Pot

Terracotta potato pots can cook up to 450 g/1 lb of whole potatoes at a time. Soak the clay pot for at least 20 minutes before use, then add even-sized, preferably smallish potatoes. Drizzle over a little olive oil and season generously with salt and freshly ground black pepper. Cover the pot with the lid and put in a cold oven, setting the temperature to 200°C/400°F/Gas Mark 6. The potatoes will take about 45 minutes to cook.

Microwaved Potatoes

This method of cooking is suitable for boiling and baking potatoes, providing you do not want the skins to be crispy. To cook new potatoes, prick the skins with a skewer to prevent them from bursting, then place in a bowl with 3 tablespoons of boiling water. Cover with clingfilm which has been pierced two or three times and cook on High for 12–15 minutes, or until tender. Peeled chunks of potato can be cooked in the same way. To bake potatoes, place each potato on a circle of kitchen paper. Make several cuts in each to ensure that the skins do not burst. Transfer to the microwave plate and cook on High for 4–6 minutes per potato, allowing an extra 3–4 minutes for every additional potato. Turn the potatoes at least once during cooking. Leave to stand for 5 minutes before serving.

Health and Nutrition

Potatoes are high in complex carbohydrates, providing sustained energy. They are also an excellent source of vitamins B and C and minerals such as iron and potassium. They contain almost no fat and are high in dietary fibre.

Soups & Light Bites

Potatoes are one of the most invaluable ingredients in those hearty, filling soups that we all love. This section includes favourites such as Potato, Leek & Rosemary Soup and traditional dishes such as Cullen Skink. The potato's versatility makes it very useful in creating all sorts of snacks, from Potato Skins to Sweet Potato Crisps with Mango Salsa. And don't forget all those tasty salads that use baby potatoes.

Sweet Potato Baps

1 Preheat the oven to 200°C/400°F/Gas Mark 6 15 minutes before baking. Peel the sweet potato and cut into large chunks. Cook in a saucepan of boiling water for 12–15 minutes, or until tender. Drain well and mash with the butter and nutmeg. Stir in the milk, then leave until barely warm.

2 Sift the flour and salt into a large bowl. Stir in the yeast. Make a well in the centre. Add the mashed sweet potato and beaten egg and mix to a soft dough. Add a little more milk if needed, depending on the moisture in the sweet potato.

3 Turn out the dough on to a lightly floured surface and knead for about 10 minutes, or until smooth and elastic. Place in a lightly oiled bowl, cover with clingfilm and leave in a warm place to rise for about 1 hour, or until the dough doubles in size. Turn out the dough and knead for a minute or two until smooth. Divide into 16 pieces, shape into rolls and place on a large oiled baking sheet. Cover with oiled clingfilm and leave to rise for 15 minutes.

4 Brush the rolls with beaten egg, then sprinkle half with rolled oats and leave the rest plain.

5 Bake in the preheated oven for 12–15 minutes, or until well risen, lightly browned and sound hollow when the bases are tapped. Transfer to a wire rack and immediately cover with a clean tea towel to keep the crusts soft.

Ingredients   MAKES 16

225 g/8 oz sweet potato
15 g/¹/₂ oz butter
freshly grated nutmeg
about 200 ml/7 fl oz milk
450 g/1 lb strong plain white flour
2 tsp salt
7 g/¹/₄ oz sachet easy-blend yeast
1 medium egg, beaten

To finish:

beaten egg, to glaze
1 tbsp rolled oats

Helpful Hint

There are many varieties of sweet potato, so be sure to choose the correct potato for this recipe as their flavours and textures vary. The sweet potato used in this recipe is dark skinned and has a vibrant orange flesh which cooks to a moist texture.

Cheese-crusted Potato Scones

1 Preheat the oven to 220°C/425°F/Gas Mark 7 15 minutes before baking. Sift the flours, salt and baking powder into a large bowl. Rub in the butter until the mixture resembles fine breadcrumbs.

2 Stir 4 tablespoons of the milk into the mashed potato and season with black pepper. Add the dry ingredients to the potato mixture, mixing together with a fork and adding the remaining 1 tablespoon of milk if needed.

3 Knead the dough on a lightly floured surface for a few seconds until smooth. Roll out to a 15 cm/6 inch round and transfer to an oiled baking sheet.

4 Mark the scone round into 6 wedges, cutting about halfway through with a small sharp knife. Brush with milk, then sprinkle with the cheese and a faint dusting of paprika. Bake on the middle shelf of the preheated oven for 15 minutes, or until well risen and golden brown.

5 Transfer to a wire rack and leave to cool for 5 minutes before breaking into wedges.

6 Serve warm or leave to cool completely. Once cool, store the scones in an airtight tin. Garnish with a sprig of basil and serve split and buttered.

Ingredients   MAKES 6

200 g/7 oz self-raising flour
25 g/1 oz wholemeal flour
$^1/_2$ tsp salt
$1^1/_2$ tsp baking powder
25 g/1 oz butter, cubed
5 tbsp milk
175 g/6 oz cold mashed potato
freshly ground black pepper

To finish:

2 tbsp milk
40 g/$1^1/_2$ oz mature Cheddar cheese, finely grated
paprika pepper, to dust
sprig of basil, to garnish

Rice Soup with Potato Sticks

1 Preheat the oven to 190°C/375°F/Gas Mark 5. Heat 25 g/1 oz of the butter and the olive oil in a saucepan and cook the onion for 4–5 minutes until softened, then add the Parma ham and cook for about 1 minute. Stir in the rice, the stock and the peas. Season to taste with salt and pepper and simmer for 10–15 minutes, or until the rice is tender.

2 Beat the egg and 125 g/4 oz of the butter together until smooth, then beat in the flour, a pinch of salt and the potato. Work the ingredients together to form a soft, pliable dough, adding a little more flour if necessary.

3 Roll the dough out on a lightly floured surface into a rectangle 1 cm/^{1}/$_2$ inch thick and cut into 12 long thin sticks. Brush with milk and sprinkle on the poppy seeds. Place the sticks on a lightly oiled baking tray and bake in the preheated oven for 15 minutes, or until golden.

4 When the rice is cooked, stir the remaining butter and Parmesan cheese into the soup and sprinkle the chopped parsley over the top. Serve immediately with the warm potato sticks.

Ingredients   SERVES 4

175 g/6 oz butter
1 tsp olive oil
1 large onion, peeled and finely chopped
4 slices Parma ham, chopped
100 g/3^1/$_2$ oz Arborio rice
1.1 litres/2 pints chicken stock
350 g/12 oz frozen peas
salt and freshly ground black pepper
1 medium egg
125 g/4 oz self-raising flour
175 g/6 oz mashed potato
1 tbsp milk
1 tbsp poppy seeds
1 tbsp Parmesan cheese, finely grated
1 tbsp freshly chopped parsley

Tasty Tip

These potato sticks also make a delicious snack with drinks. Try sprinkling them with sesame seeds or grated cheese and allow to cool before serving.

Rocket & Potato Soup with Garlic Croutons

1 Place the potatoes in a large saucepan, cover with the stock and simmer gently for 10 minutes. Add the rocket leaves and simmer for a further 5–10 minutes, or until the potatoes are soft and the rocket has wilted.

2 Meanwhile, make the croutons. Cut the thick, white sliced bread into small cubes and reserve. Heat the butter and groundnut oil in a small frying pan and cook the garlic for 1 minute, stirring well. Remove the garlic. Add the bread cubes to the butter and oil mixture in the frying pan and sauté, stirring continuously, until they are golden brown. Drain the croutons on absorbent kitchen paper and reserve.

3 Cut the ciabatta bread into small dice and stir into the soup. Cover the saucepan and leave to stand for 10 minutes, or until the bread has absorbed a lot of the liquid.

4 Stir in the olive oil, season to taste with salt and pepper and serve at once with a few of the garlic croutons scattered over the top and a little grated Parmesan cheese.

Ingredients   SERVES 4

700 g/1¹/₂ lb baby new potatoes
1.1 litres/2 pints chicken or
   vegetable stock
50 g/2 oz rocket leaves
125 g/4 oz thick, white sliced bread
50 g/2 oz unsalted butter
1 tsp groundnut oil
2–4 garlic cloves, peeled and
   chopped
125 g/4 oz stale ciabatta bread,
   crusts removed
4 tbsp olive oil
salt and freshly ground black pepper
2 tbsp Parmesan cheese,
   finely grated

Helpful Hint

Rocket is now widely available in bags from most large supermarkets. If, however, you cannot get hold of it, replace it with an equal quantity of watercress or baby spinach leaves.

Swede, Turnip, Parsnip & Potato Soup

1 Finely chop 1 onion. Melt the butter in a large saucepan and add the onion, carrots, swede, turnip, parsnip and potatoes. Cover and cook gently for about 10 minutes, without colouring. Stir occasionally during this time.

2 Add the stock and season to taste with the nutmeg, salt and pepper. Cover and bring to the boil, then reduce the heat and simmer gently for 15–20 minutes, or until the vegetables are tender. Remove from the heat and leave to cool for 30 minutes.

3 Heat the oil in a large, heavy-based frying pan. Add the onions and cook over a medium heat for about 2–3 minutes, stirring frequently, until golden brown. Remove the onions with a slotted spoon and drain well on absorbent kitchen paper. As they cool, they will turn crispy.

4 Pour the cooled soup into a food processor or blender and process to form a smooth purée. Return to the cleaned pan, adjust the seasoning, then stir in the cream. Gently reheat and top with the crispy onions. Serve immediately with chunks of bread.

Ingredients   SERVES 4

2 large onions, peeled
25 g/1 oz butter
2 medium carrots, peeled and
  roughly chopped
175 g/6 oz swede, peeled and
  roughly chopped
125 g/4 oz turnip, peeled and
  roughly chopped
125 g/4 oz parsnips, peeled and
  roughly chopped
175 g/6 oz potatoes, peeled
1 litre/1³/₄ pints vegetable stock
¹/₂ tsp freshly grated nutmeg
salt and freshly ground black pepper
4 tbsp vegetable oil, for frying
125 ml/4 fl oz double cream
warm crusty bread, to serve

Helpful Hint

For a lower-fat version of this delicious soup, add milk (skimmed if preferred) rather than cream when reheating.

Potato & Fennel Soup

1 Melt the butter in a large, heavy-based saucepan. Add the onions with the garlic and half the salt and cook over a medium heat, stirring occasionally, for 7–10 minutes, or until the onions are very soft and beginning to turn brown.

2 Add the potatoes, fennel bulb, caraway seeds and the remaining salt. Cook for about 5 minutes, then pour in the vegetable stock. Bring to the boil, partially cover and simmer for 15–20 minutes, or until the potatoes are tender. Stir in the chopped parsley and adjust the seasoning to taste.

3 For a smooth-textured soup, allow to cool slightly, then pour into a food processor or blender and blend until smooth. Reheat the soup gently, then ladle into individual soup bowls. For a chunky soup, omit this blending stage and ladle straight from the saucepan into soup bowls.

4 Swirl a spoonful of crème fraîche into each bowl and serve immediately with roughly-torn pieces of French stick.

Ingredients   SERVES 4

25 g/1 oz butter
2 large onions, peeled and thinly sliced
2–3 garlic cloves, peeled and crushed
1 tsp salt
2 medium potatoes (about 450 g/1 lb in weight), peeled and diced
1 fennel bulb, trimmed and finely chopped
$^1/_2$ tsp caraway seeds
1 litre/1$^3/_4$ pints vegetable stock
freshly ground black pepper
2 tbsp freshly chopped parsley
4 tbsp crème fraîche
roughly torn pieces of French stick, to serve

Food Fact

Fennel has a distinct aniseed flavour, which mellows and sweetens when cooked. Look out for well-rounded bulbs with bright green fronds. Fennel is at its best when fresh, so should be used as soon as possible after buying. It may be stored in the salad drawer of the refrigerator for a few days.

Potatoes, Leek & Rosemary Soup

1 Melt the butter in a large saucepan, add the leeks and cook gently for 5 minutes, stirring frequently. Remove 1 tablespoon of the cooked leeks and reserve for garnishing.

2 Add the potatoes, vegetable stock, rosemary sprigs and milk. Bring to the boil, then reduce the heat, cover and simmer gently for 20–25 minutes, or until the vegetables are tender.

3 Cool for 10 minutes. Discard the rosemary, then pour into a food processor or blender and blend well to form a smooth-textured soup.

4 Return the soup to the cleaned saucepan and stir in the chopped parsley and crème fraîche. Season to taste with salt and pepper. If the soup is too thick, stir in a little more milk or water. Reheat gently without boiling, then ladle into warm soup bowls. Garnish the soup with the reserved leeks and serve immediately with wholemeal rolls.

Ingredients   SERVES 4

50 g/2 oz butter
450 g/1 lb leeks, trimmed and
    finely sliced
700 g/1¹/₂ lb potatoes, peeled and
    roughly chopped
900 ml/1¹/₂ pints vegetable stock
4 sprigs fresh rosemary
450 ml/³/₄ pint full-cream milk
2 tbsp freshly chopped parsley
2 tbsp crème fraîche
salt and freshly ground black pepper
wholemeal rolls, to serve

Tasty Tip

This rosemary-scented version of vichyssoise is equally delicious served cold. Allow the soup to cool before covering, then chill in the refrigerator for at least 2 hours. The soup will thicken as it chills, so you may need to thin it to the desired consistency with more milk or stock and season before serving. It is important to use fresh rosemary for this recipe.

Cream of Spinach Soup

1 Place the onion, garlic and potatoes in a large saucepan and cover with the cold water. Add half the salt and bring to the boil. Cover and simmer for 15–20 minutes, or until the potatoes are tender. Remove from the heat and add the spinach. Cover and set aside for 10 minutes.

2 Slowly melt the butter in another saucepan, add the flour and cook over a low heat for about 2 minutes. Remove the saucepan from the heat and add the milk, a little at a time, stirring continuously. Return to the heat and cook, stirring continuously, for 5–8 minutes, or until the sauce is smooth and slightly thickened. Add the freshly grated nutmeg.

3 Blend the cooled potato and spinach mixture in a food processor or blender to a smooth purée, then return to the saucepan and gradually stir in the white sauce. Season to taste with salt and pepper and gently reheat, taking care not to allow the soup to boil. Ladle into soup bowls and top with spoonfuls of crème fraîche or soured cream. Serve immediately with warm foccacia bread.

Ingredients   SERVES 4

1 large onion, peeled and chopped
5 large plump garlic cloves, peeled
    and chopped
2 medium potatoes, peeled and
    chopped
750 ml/1¹/₄ pints cold water
1 tsp salt
450 g/1 lb spinach, washed and large
    stems removed
50 g/2 oz butter
3 tbsp flour
750 ml/1¹/₄ pints milk
¹/₂ tsp freshly grated nutmeg, or to taste
freshly ground black pepper
6–8 tbsp crème fraîche or soured cream
warm foccacia bread, to serve

Helpful Hint

When choosing spinach, always look for fresh, crisp, dark green leaves. Use within 1–2 days of buying and store in a cool place until needed. To prepare, wash in several changes of water to remove any dirt or grit and shake off as much excess water as possible.

Pumpkin & Smoked Haddock Soup

1 Heat the oil in a large, heavy-based saucepan and gently cook the onion, garlic and celery for about 10 minutes. This will release the sweetness but not colour the vegetables. Add the pumpkin and potatoes to the saucepan and stir to coat the vegetables with the oil.

2 Gradually pour in the stock and bring to the boil. Cover, then reduce the heat and simmer for 25 minutes, stirring occasionally. Stir in the dry sherry, then remove the saucepan from the heat and leave to cool for 5–10 minutes.

3 Blend the mixture in a food processor or blender to form a chunky purée and return to the cleaned saucepan.

4 Meanwhile, place the fish in a shallow frying pan. Pour in the milk with 3 tablespoons of water and bring to almost boiling point. Reduce the heat, cover and simmer for 6 minutes, or until the fish is cooked and flakes easily. Remove from the heat and, using a slotted spoon, remove the fish from the liquid, reserving both liquid and fish.

5 Discard the skin and any bones from the fish and flake into pieces. Stir the fish liquid into the soup, together with the flaked fish. Season with freshly ground black pepper, stir in the parsley and serve immediately.

Ingredients   SERVES 4–6

2 tbsp olive oil
1 medium onion, peeled and
    chopped
2 garlic cloves, peeled and chopped
3 celery sticks, trimmed and chopped
700 g/1½ lb pumpkin, peeled,
    deseeded and cut into chunks
450 g/1 lb potatoes, peeled and cut
    into chunks
750 ml/1¼ pints chicken stock,
    heated
125 ml/4 fl oz dry sherry
200 g/7 oz smoked haddock fillet
150 ml/¼ pint milk
freshly ground black pepper
2 tbsp freshly chopped parsley

Tasty Tip

Try to find undyed smoked haddock for this soup rather than the brightly coloured yellow type, as the texture and flavour are better.

Mediterranean Chowder

1 Heat the oil and butter together in a large saucepan, add the onion, celery and garlic and cook gently for 2–3 minutes until softened. Add the chilli and stir in the flour. Cook, stirring, for a further minute.

2 Add the potatoes to the saucepan with the stock. Bring to the boil, cover and simmer for 10 minutes. Add the fish cubes to the saucepan with the chopped parsley and cook for a further 5–10 minutes, or until the fish and potatoes are just tender.

3 Stir in the peeled prawns and sweetcorn and season to taste with salt and pepper. Pour in the cream and adjust the seasoning if necessary.

4 Scatter the snipped chives over the top of the chowder. Ladle into 6 large bowls and serve immediately with plenty of warm crusty bread.

Ingredients   SERVES 6

1 tbsp olive oil
1 tbsp butter
1 large onion, peeled and finely sliced
4 celery sticks, trimmed and
   thinly sliced
2 garlic cloves, peeled and crushed
1 bird's eye chilli, deseeded and
   finely chopped
1 tbsp plain flour
225 g/8 oz potatoes, peeled and diced
600 ml/1 pint fish or vegetable stock
700 g/1 1/2 lb whiting or cod fillet, cut
   into 2.5 cm/1 inch cubes
2 tbsp freshly chopped parsley
125 g/4 oz large peeled prawns
198 g can sweetcorn, drained
salt and freshly ground black pepper
150 ml/1/4 pint single cream
1 tbsp freshly snipped chives
warm crusty bread, to serve

Cullen Skink

1 Melt the butter in a large, heavy-based saucepan, add the onion and sauté for 3 minutes, stirring occasionally. Add the bay leaf and stir, then sprinkle in the flour and cook over a low heat for 2 minutes, stirring frequently. Add the potatoes.

2 Take off the heat and gradually stir in the milk and water. Return to the heat and bring to the boil, stirring. Reduce the heat to a simmer and cook for 10 minutes.

3 Meanwhile, discard any pin bones from the fish and cut into small pieces. Add to the pan, together with the sweetcorn and peas. Cover and cook gently, stirring occasionally, for 10 minutes, or until the vegetables and fish are cooked.

4 Add pepper and nutmeg to taste, then stir in the cream and heat gently for 1–2 minutes, or until piping hot. Sprinkle with the parsley and serve with crusty bread.

Ingredients
SERVES 4

25 g/1 oz unsalted butter
1 onion, peeled and chopped
1 fresh bay leaf
25 g/1 oz plain flour
350 g/12 oz new potatoes, scrubbed and cut into small pieces
600 ml/1 pint semi-skimmed milk
300 ml/$^1/_2$ pint water
350 g/12 oz undyed smoked haddock fillet, skinned
75 g/3 oz sweetcorn kernels
50 g/2 oz garden peas
freshly ground black pepper
$^1/_2$ tsp freshly grated nutmeg
2–3 tbsp single cream
2 tbsp freshly chopped parsley
crusty bread, to serve

Tasty Tip
Add 100 g/3$^1/_2$ oz raw peeled prawns with the cream, if liked. Take care not to overcook or the prawns will lose their flavour and will be tough.

Cawl

1 Put the lamb in a large saucepan, cover with cold water and bring to the boil. Add a generous pinch of salt. Simmer gently for 1½ hours, then set aside to cool completely, preferably overnight.

2 The next day, skim the fat off the surface of the lamb liquid and discard. Return the saucepan to the heat and bring back to the boil. Simmer for 5 minutes. Add the onions, potatoes, parsnips, swede and carrots and return to the boil. Reduce the heat, cover and cook for about 20 minutes, stirring occasionally.

3 Add the leeks and season to taste with salt and pepper. Cook for a further 10 minutes, or until all the vegetables are tender.

4 Using a slotted spoon, remove the meat from the saucepan and take the meat off the bone. Discard the bones and any gristle, then return the meat to the pan. Adjust the seasoning to taste, stir in the parsley, then serve immediately with plenty of warm crusty bread.

Ingredients   SERVES 4–6

700 g/1½ lb scrag end of lamb or best
    end of neck chops
pinch of salt
2 large onions, peeled and thinly sliced
3 large potatoes, peeled and cut
    into chunks
2 parsnips, peeled and cut into chunks
1 swede, peeled and cut into chunks
3 large carrots, peeled and cut
    into chunks
2 leeks, trimmed and sliced
freshly ground black pepper
4 tbsp freshly chopped parsley
warm crusty bread, to serve

Food Fact

Many traditional Welsh recipes such as Cawl feature lamb. This flavoursome soup was once a staple dish, originally made with scraps of mutton or lamb and vegetables cooked together in a broth.

Pasta & Bean Soup

1 Heat the olive oil in a heavy-based pan, add the celery and prosciutto and cook gently for 6–8 minutes, or until softened. Add the chopped chilli and potato cubes and cook for a further 10 minutes.

2 Add the garlic to the chilli and potato mixture and cook for 1 minute. Add the chopped tomatoes and simmer for 5 minutes. Stir in two thirds of the beans, then pour in the chicken or vegetable stock and bring to the boil.

3 Add the pasta shapes to the soup stock and return it to simmering point. Cook the pasta for about 10 minutes, or until *al dente*.

4 Meanwhile, place the remaining beans in a food processor or blender and blend with enough of the soup stock to make a smooth, thinnish purée.

5 When the pasta is cooked, stir in the puréed beans with the torn basil. Season the soup to taste with salt and pepper. Ladle into serving bowls, garnish with shredded basil and serve immediately with plenty of crusty bread.

Ingredients   SERVES 4–6

3 tbsp olive oil
2 celery sticks, trimmed and
    finely chopped
100 g/3$^{1}/_{2}$ oz prosciutto or prosciutto
    di speck, cut into pieces
1 red chilli, deseeded and finely
    chopped
2 large potatoes, peeled and cut
    into 2.5 cm/1 in cubes
2 garlic cloves, peeled and finely
    chopped
3 ripe plum tomatoes, skinned
    and chopped
1 x 400 g cans borlotti beans,
    drained and rinsed
1 litre/1$^{3}/_{4}$ pints chicken
    or vegetable stock
100 g/3$^{1}/_{2}$ oz pasta shapes
large handful basil leaves, torn
salt and freshly ground black pepper
shredded basil leaves, to garnish
crusty bread, to serve

Gnocchi with Grilled Cherry Tomato Sauce

1 Preheat the grill just before required. Bring a large pan of salted water to the boil, add the potatoes and cook for 20–25 minutes until tender. Drain. Leave until cool enough to handle but still hot, then peel them and place in a large bowl. Mash until smooth, then work in the egg, salt and enough of the flour to form a soft dough.

2 With floured hands, roll a spoonful of the dough into a small ball. Flatten it slightly on to the back of a large fork to make a little ridged dumpling. Repeat with the rest of the dough. Place each gnocchi on to a floured tea towel as you work.

3 Place the tomatoes in a flameproof shallow dish. Add the garlic, lemon zest, herbs and olive oil. Season to taste with salt and pepper and sprinkle over the sugar. Cook under the preheated grill for 10 minutes, or until the tomatoes are charred and tender, stirring once or twice.

4 Meanwhile, bring a large pan of lightly salted water to the boil, then reduce to a steady simmer. Dropping in 6–8 gnocchi at a time, cook in batches for 3–4 minutes, or until they begin bobbing up to the surface. Remove with a slotted spoon and drain well on absorbent kitchen paper before transferring to a warmed serving dish; cover with foil. Toss the cooked gnocchi with the tomato sauce. Serve immediately with a little grated Parmesan cheese.

Ingredients SERVES 4

450 g/1 lb floury potatoes, unpeeled
1 medium egg
1 tsp salt
75–90 g/3–3$\frac{1}{2}$ oz plain flour
450 g/1 lb mixed red and orange
   cherry tomatoes, halved lengthways
2 garlic cloves, peeled and
   finely sliced
zest of $\frac{1}{2}$ lemon, finely grated
1 tbsp freshly chopped thyme
1 tbsp freshly chopped basil
2 tbsp extra virgin olive oil, plus extra
   for drizzling
salt and freshly ground black pepper
pinch of sugar
freshly grated Parmesan cheese,
   to serve

Helpful Hint

When cooking the gnocchi, use a very large pan with at least 1.7 litres/3 pints of water to give them plenty of room so that they do not stick together.

Spaghetti with Fresh Tomatoes, Chilli & Potatoes

1 Preheat the grill to high 5 minutes before using. Cook the potatoes in plenty of boiling water until tender but firm. Allow to cool, then peel and cut into cubes.

2 Blend the garlic, basil and 4 tablespoons of the olive oil in a blender or food processor until the basil is finely chopped, then reserve.

3 Place the tomatoes with the basil and oil mixture in a small bowl, add the chilli and season to taste with salt and pepper. Mix together and reserve the sauce.

4 Bring a large pan of salted water to a rolling boil, add the spaghetti and cook according to the packet instructions, or until *al dente*.

5 Meanwhile, toss the potato cubes with the remaining olive oil and transfer to a baking sheet. Place the potatoes under the preheated grill until they are crisp and golden, turning once or twice, then drain on absorbent kitchen paper.

6 Drain the pasta thoroughly and transfer to a warmed shallow serving bowl. Add the tomato sauce and the hot potatoes. Toss well and adjust the seasoning to taste. Serve immediately with the grated Parmesan cheese, if using.

Ingredients   SERVES 6

2 medium potatoes, unpeeled
3 garlic cloves, peeled and crushed
1 small bunch basil, roughly chopped
6 tbsp olive oil
4 large ripe plum tomatoes, skinned, deseeded and chopped
1 small red chilli, deseeded and finely chopped
salt and freshly ground black pepper
450 g/1 lb spaghetti
4 tbsp freshly grated Parmesan cheese, to serve (optional)

Pasta Genovese with Pesto, Green Beans & Potatoes

1 Put the basil leaves, garlic, pine nuts and Parmesan cheese into a food processor and blend until finely chopped. Transfer the mixture into a small bowl and stir in the extra virgn olive oil. Season the pesto to taste with salt and pepper and reserve.

2 Bring a pan of salted water to the boil and cook the potatoes for 12–14 minutes, or until tender. About 4 minutes before the end of the cooking time, add the beans. Drain well and refresh under cold water. Reserve the beans and slice the potatoes thickly, or halve them if small.

3 Heat the olive oil in a frying pan and add the potatoes. Fry over a medium heat for 5 minutes, or until golden. Add the reserved beans and pesto and cook for a further 2 minutes.

4 Meanwhile, bring a large pan of lightly salted water to a rolling boil. Cook the pasta shapes according to the packet instructions, or until *al dente*. Drain thoroughly, return to the pan and add the potato mixture. Toss well and heat through for 1–2 minutes. Tip into a warmed serving bowl and serve immediately with Parmesan cheese.

Ingredients   SERVES 6

40 g/1¹/₂ oz basil leaves
2 garlic cloves, peeled and crushed
2 tbsp pine nuts, lightly toasted
25 g/1 oz freshly grated Parmesan cheese
75 ml/3 fl oz extra virgin olive oil
salt and freshly ground black pepper
175 g/6 oz new potatoes, scrubbed
125 g/4 oz fine French beans, trimmed
2 tbsp olive oil
450 g/1 lb pasta shapes
extra freshly grated Parmesan cheese, to serve

Tasty Tip

Classic pesto, as used in this recipe, is always made with fresh basil and pine nuts, but other herb variations work equally well. For a change, try a coriander and chilli pesto, replacing the basil with fresh coriander leaves and adding a deseeded and finely chopped red chilli.

Courgette & Tarragon Tortilla

1 Peel the potatoes and slice thinly. Dry the slices in a clean tea towel to get them as dry as possible. Heat the oil in a large, heavy-based pan, add the onion and cook for 3 minutes. Add the potatoes with a little salt and pepper, then stir the potatoes and onion lightly to coat in the oil.

2 Reduce the heat to the lowest possible setting, cover and cook gently for 5 minutes. Turn the potatoes and onion over and continue to cook for a further 5 minutes. Give the pan a shake every now and again to ensure that the potatoes do not stick to the base or burn. Add the courgette, then cover and cook for a further 10 minutes.

3 Beat the eggs and tarragon together and season to taste with salt and pepper. Pour the egg mixture over the vegetables and return to the heat. Cook on a low heat for up to 20–25 minutes, or until there is no liquid egg left on the surface of the tortilla.

4 Turn the tortilla over by inverting it onto the lid or onto a flat plate. Return the pan to the heat and cook for a final 3–5 minutes, or until the underside is golden brown. If preferred, place the tortilla under a preheated grill for 4 minutes, or until set and golden brown on top. Cut into small squares and serve hot or cold with tomato wedges.

Ingredients SERVES 6

700 g/1¹/₂ lb potatoes
3 tbsp olive oil
1 onion, peeled and thinly sliced
salt and freshly ground black pepper
1 courgette, trimmed and
   thinly sliced
6 medium eggs
2 tbsp freshly chopped tarragon
tomato wedges, to serve

Food Fact

Almost regarded as the national dish of Spain, this substantial omelette is traditionally made from eggs, potatoes and onions. Here, courgettes and tarragon are added for extra flavour and colour. Use even-sized waxy potatoes, which will not break up during cooking – Maris Bard, Charlotte or Pentland Javelin are all good choices of potato.

Special Rosti

1 Cook the potatoes in a large saucepan of salted boiling water for about 10 minutes, until just tender. Drain in a colander, then rinse in cold water. Drain again. Leave until cool enough to handle, then peel off the skins.

2 Melt the butter in a large frying pan and gently fry the onion and garlic for about 3 minutes until softened and beginning to colour. Remove from the heat.

3 Coarsely grate the potatoes into a large bowl, then stir in the onion and garlic mixture. Sprinkle over the parsley and stir well to mix. Season to taste with salt and pepper.

4 Heat the oil in the frying pan and cover the base of the pan with half the potato mixture. Lay the slices of Parma ham on top. Sprinkle with the chopped sun-dried tomatoes, then scatter the grated Emmenthal over the top.

5 Finally, top with the remaining potato mixture. Cook over a low heat, pressing down with a palette knife from time to time, for 10–15 minutes, or until the bottom is golden brown. Carefully invert the rosti onto a large plate, then carefully slide back into the pan and cook the other side until golden. Serve cut into wedges with a mixed green salad.

Ingredients   SERVES 4

700 g/1¹/₂ lb potatoes, scrubbed but not peeled
salt and freshly ground black pepper
75 g/3 oz butter
1 large onion, peeled and finely chopped
1 garlic clove, peeled and crushed
2 tbsp freshly chopped parsley
1 tbsp olive oil
75 g/3 oz Parma ham, thinly sliced
50 g/2 oz sun-dried tomatoes, chopped
175 g/6 oz Emmenthal cheese, grated
mixed green salad, to serve

Helpful Hint

To make sure the rosti is the right thickness, you will need a heavy-based nonstick frying pan with a diameter of about 23 cm/9 inches.

Potato & Goats' Cheese Tart

1 Preheat the oven to 190°C/375°F/Gas Mark 5, about 10 minutes before cooking. Roll the pastry out on a lightly floured surface and use to line a 23 cm/9 inch fluted flan tin. Chill in the refrigerator for 30 minutes.

2 Scrub the potatoes, place in a large saucepan of lightly salted water and bring to the boil. Simmer for 10–15 minutes, or until the potatoes are tender. Drain and reserve until cool enough to handle.

3 Line the pastry case with greaseproof paper and baking beans or crumpled foil and bake blind in the preheated oven for 15 minutes. Remove from the oven and discard the paper and beans or foil. Brush the base with a little beaten egg, then return to the oven and cook for a further 5 minutes. Remove from the oven.

4 Cut the potatoes into 1 cm/½ inch thick slices; reserve. Spread the sun-dried tomato paste over the base of the pastry case, sprinkle with the chilli powder, then arrange the potato slices on top in a decorative pattern.

5 Beat together the egg, soured cream, milk and chives, then season to taste with salt and pepper. Pour over the potatoes. Arrange the goats' cheese on top of the potatoes. Bake in the preheated oven for 30 minutes until golden brown and set. Serve immediately with salad and warm crusty bread.

Ingredients   SERVES 6

275 g/10 oz prepared shortcrust
  pastry, thawed if frozen
550 g/1¼ lb small waxy potatoes
salt and freshly ground black pepper
beaten egg, for brushing
2 tbsp sun-dried tomato paste
¼ tsp chilli powder, or to taste
1 large egg
150 ml/¼ pint soured cream
150 ml/¼ pint milk
2 tbsp freshly snipped chives
300 g/11 oz goats' cheese, sliced
salad and warm crusty bread,
  to serve

Helpful Hint

Using bought ready-made shortcrust pastry is a good way to save time, but always remove it from the refrigerator 10–15 minutes before rolling out, otherwise it may be difficult to handle. Brushing the base with egg helps seal the pastry and keeps it crisp when filled.

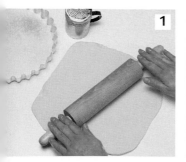

Potato Pancakes

1   To make the sauce, mix together the crème fraîche, horseradish, lime rind and juice and chives. Cover and reserve.

2   Place the potatoes in a large saucepan and cover with lightly salted boiling water. Bring back to the boil, cover and simmer for 15 minutes, or until the potatoes are tender. Drain and mash until smooth. Cool for 5 minutes, then whisk in the egg white, milk, flour, thyme and salt to form a thick, smooth batter. Leave to stand for 30 minutes, then stir before using.

3   Heat a little oil in a heavy-based frying pan. Add 2–3 large spoonfuls of batter to make a small pancake and cook for 1–2 minutes until golden. Flip the pancake and cook for a further minute, or until golden. Repeat with the remaining batter to make 8 pancakes.

4   Arrange the pancakes on a plate and top with the smoked mackerel. Garnish with herbs and serve immediately with spoonfuls of the reserved horseradish sauce.

Ingredients   SERVES 6

For the sauce:

4 tbsp crème fraîche
1 tbsp horseradish sauce
grated rind and juice of 1 lime
1 tbsp freshly snipped chives

225 g/8 oz floury potatoes, peeled and cut into chunks
1 small egg white
2 tbsp milk
2 tsp self-raising flour
1 tbsp freshly chopped thyme
large pinch of salt
a little vegetable oil, for frying
225 g/8 oz smoked mackerel fillets, skinned and roughly chopped
fresh herbs, to garnish

Helpful Hint

Keep the pancakes warm as you make them by stacking on a warmed plate. Place greaseproof paper between each pancake to keep them separate and fold a clean tea towel loosely over the top.

Sweet Potato Crisps with Mango Salsa

1 To make the salsa, mix the mango with the tomatoes, cucumber and onion. Add the sugar, chilli, vinegar, oil and the lime rind and juice. Mix together thoroughly, cover and leave for 45–50 minutes.

2 Soak the potatoes in cold water for 40 minutes to remove as much of the excess starch as possible. Drain and dry thoroughly in a clean tea towel or absorbent kitchen paper.

3 Heat the oil to 190°C/375°F in a deep fryer. When at the correct temperature, place half the potatoes in the frying basket, then carefully lower the potatoes into the hot oil and cook for 4–5 minutes, or until they are golden brown, shaking the basket every minute so that they do not stick together.

4 Drain the potato crisps on absorbent kitchen paper, sprinkle with sea salt and place under a preheated moderate grill for a few seconds to dry out. Repeat with the remaining potatoes. Stir the mint into the salsa and serve with the potato crisps.

Ingredients   SERVES 6

For the salsa:

1 large mango, peeled, stoned and
   cut into small cubes
8 cherry tomatoes, quartered
1/2 cucumber, peeled if preferred and
   finely diced
1 red onion, peeled and finely chopped
pinch of sugar
1 red chilli, deseeded and finely chopped
2 tbsp rice vinegar
2 tbsp olive oil
grated rind and juice of 1 lime

450 g/1 lb sweet potatoes, peeled and
   thinly sliced
vegetable oil, for deep frying
sea salt
2 tbsp freshly chopped mint

Helpful Hint

Take care when deep-frying. Use a deep, heavy-based saucepan or special deep fryer and fill the pan no more than one-third full with oil.

Potato Skins

1 Preheat the oven to 200°C/400°F/Gas Mark 6. Scrub the potatoes, then prick a few times with a fork or skewer and place directly on the top shelf of the oven. Bake in the preheated oven for at least 1 hour, or until tender. The potatoes are cooked when they yield gently to the pressure of your hand.

2 Set the potatoes aside until cool enough to handle, then cut in half and scoop the flesh into a bowl and reserve. Preheat the grill and line the grill rack with foil.

3 Mix together the oil and the paprika and use half to brush the outside of the potato skins. Place on the grill rack under the preheated hot grill and cook for 5 minutes, or until crisp, turning as necessary.

4 Heat the remaining paprika-flavoured oil and gently fry the pancetta until crisp. Add to the potato flesh along with the cream, Gorgonzola cheese and parsley. Halve the potato skins and fill with the Gorgonzola filling. Return to the oven for a further 15 minutes to heat through. Sprinkle with a little more paprika and serve immediately with mayonnaise, sweet chilli sauce and a green salad.

Ingredients   SERVES 4

4 large baking potatoes
2 tbsp olive oil
2 tsp paprika
125 g/4 oz pancetta, roughly
   chopped
6 tbsp double cream
125 g/4 oz Gorgonzola cheese
1 tbsp freshly chopped parsley

To serve:

reduced-calorie mayonnaise
sweet chilli dipping sauce
tossed green salad

Food Fact

Now mostly produced in Lombardy, Gorgonzola is made from pasteurised cows' milk and allowed to ripen for at least 3 months, giving it a rich but not overpowering flavour. Unlike most blue cheeses, it should have a greater concentration of veining towards the centre of the cheese.

Ginger & Garlic Potatoes

1 Scrub the potatoes, then place, unpeeled, in a large saucepan and cover with boiling salted water. Bring to the boil and cook for 15 minutes, then drain and leave the potatoes to cool completely. Peel and cut into 2.5 cm/1 inch cubes.

2 Place the root ginger, garlic, turmeric, salt and cayenne pepper in a food processor and blend for 1 minute. With the motor still running, slowly add 3 tablespoons of water and blend into a paste. Alternatively, pound the ingredients to a paste with a pestle and mortar.

3 Heat the oil in a large, heavy-based frying pan and, when hot but not smoking, add the fennel seeds and fry for a few minutes. Stir in the ginger paste and cook for 2 minutes, stirring frequently. Take care not to burn the mixture.

4 Reduce the heat, then add the potatoes and cook for 5–7 minutes, stirring frequently, until the potatoes have a golden-brown crust. Add the diced apple and spring onions, then sprinkle with the freshly chopped coriander. Heat through for 2 minutes, then serve on assorted salad leaves with curry-flavoured mayonnaise.

Ingredients SERVES 4

700 g/1½ lb potatoes
2.5 cm/1 inch piece root ginger, peeled and coarsely chopped
3 garlic cloves, peeled and chopped
½ tsp turmeric
1 tsp salt
½ tsp cayenne pepper
5 tbsp vegetable oil
1 tsp whole fennel seeds
1 large eating apple, cored and diced
6 spring onions, trimmed and diagonally sliced
1 tbsp freshly chopped coriander

To serve:

assorted bitter salad leaves
curry-flavoured mayonnaise

Food Fact

Turmeric is a rhizome that comes from the same family as ginger. When the root is dried, it has a dull yellow appearance and can be ground to a powder. It has a warm spicy flavour and gives food a wonderful golden colour.

Warm Potato, Pear & Pecan Salad

1   Scrub the potatoes, then cook in a saucepan of lightly salted boiling water for 15 minutes, or until tender. Drain, cut into halves, or quarters if large, and place in a serving bowl.

2   In a small bowl or jug, whisk together the mustard and vinegar. Gradually add the oils until the mixture begins to thicken. Stir in the poppy seeds and season to taste with salt and pepper.

3   Pour about two-thirds of the dressing over the hot potatoes and toss gently to coat. Leave until the potatoes have soaked up the dressing and are just warm.

4   Meanwhile, quarter and core the pears. Cut into thin slices, then sprinkle with the lemon juice to prevent them from going brown. Add to the potatoes with the spinach leaves and toasted pecan nuts. Gently mix together.

5   Drizzle the remaining dressing over the salad. Serve immediately before the spinach starts to wilt.

Ingredients   SERVES 4

900 g/2 lb new potatoes, preferably
    red-skinned, unpeeled
salt and freshly ground black pepper
1 tsp Dijon mustard
2 tsp white wine vinegar
3 tbsp groundnut oil
1 tbsp hazelnut or walnut oil
2 tsp poppy seeds
2 firm, ripe dessert pears
2 tsp lemon juice
175 g/6 oz baby spinach leaves
75 g/3 oz toasted pecan nuts

Handy Hint

To toast the pecan nuts, place on a baking tray in a single layer and cook in a preheated oven at 180°C/350°F/Gas Mark 4 for 5 minutes, or under a medium grill for 3–4 minutes, turning frequently. Watch them carefully – they burn easily. If you cannot get red-skinned new potatoes for this dish, add colour by using red-skinned pears instead. Look out for Red Bartlett, Red Williams and Napolian.

Mediterranean Potato Salad

1 Preheat the oven to 200°C/400°F/Gas Mark 6. Place the potatoes in a large saucepan of salted water, bring to the boil and simmer until just tender. Do not overcook. Drain and plunge into cold water to stop them from cooking further.

2 Place the onions in a bowl with the yellow and green peppers, then pour over 2 tablespoons of the olive oil. Stir and spoon onto a large baking tray. Cook in the preheated oven for 25–30 minutes, or until the vegetables are tender and lightly charred in places, stirring occasionally. Remove from the oven and transfer to a large bowl.

3 Cut the potatoes into bite-size pieces and mix with the roasted onions and peppers. Add the tomatoes and olives to the potatoes. Crumble over the feta cheese and sprinkle with the chopped parsley.

4 Whisk together the remaining olive oil, vinegar, mustard and honey, then season to taste with salt and pepper. Pour the dressing over the potatoes and toss gently together. Garnish with parsley sprigs and serve immediately.

Ingredients SERVES 4

700 g/1½ lb small waxy potatoes
2 red onions, peeled and roughly chopped
1 yellow pepper, deseeded and roughly chopped
1 green pepper, deseeded and roughly chopped
6 tbsp extra virgin olive oil
125 g/4 oz ripe tomatoes, chopped
50 g/2 oz pitted black olives, sliced
125 g/4 oz feta cheese
3 tbsp freshly chopped parsley
2 tbsp white wine vinegar
1 tsp Dijon mustard
1 tsp clear honey
salt and freshly ground black pepper
sprigs of fresh parsley, to garnish

Fish & Seafood

Fish and potatoes are perfect partners, as the dishes here reveal. We have included a fantastic version of the Traditional Fish Pie, and who needs to go to the chip shop when you could make your own Battered Cod & Chunky Chips at home? For a quick fish fix, Bombay Tuna Patties or Salmon Fish Cakes might do the trick. Dinner party dilemmas can easily be solved with the supreme Scallop & Potato Gratin or Smoked Salmon Quiche.

Smoked Haddock Rosti

1 Dry the grated potatoes in a clean tea towel. Rinse the grated onion thoroughly in cold water, dry in a clean tea towel and add to the potatoes.

2 Stir the garlic into the potato mixture. Skin the smoked haddock and remove as many of the tiny pin bones as possible. Cut into thin slices and reserve.

3 Heat the oil in a nonstick frying pan. Add half the potatoes and press well down in the frying pan. Season to taste with salt and pepper.

4 Add a layer of fish and a sprinkling of lemon rind, parsley and a little black pepper.

5 Top with the remaining potatoes and press down firmly. Cover with a sheet of foil and cook on the lowest heat for 25–30 minutes.

6 Preheat the grill 2–3 minutes before the end of the cooking time. Remove the foil and place the rosti under the grill to brown. Turn out on to a warmed serving dish and serve immediately with spoonfuls of crème fraîche, lemon wedges and mixed salad leaves.

Ingredients   SERVES 4

450 g/1 lb potatoes, peeled and
   coarsely grated
1 large onion, peeled and
   coarsely grated
2–3 garlic cloves, peeled and crushed
450 g/1 lb smoked haddock
1 tbsp olive oil
salt and freshly ground black pepper
finely grated rind of $\frac{1}{2}$ lemon
1 tbsp freshly chopped parsley
2 tbsp half-fat crème fraîche
mixed salad leaves, to garnish
lemon wedges, to serve

Helpful Hint

Use smoked haddock fillets. Finnan or Arbroath smokies would be too bony for this dish.

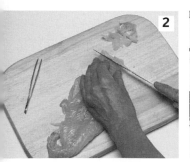

Tuna Fish Burgers

1 Place the potatoes in a large saucepan, cover with boiling water and simmer until soft. Drain, then mash with 40 g/1¹/₂ oz of the butter and the milk. Turn into a large bowl. Drain the tuna, discarding the oil and flake into the bowl of potato. Stir well to mix.

2 Add the spring onions and parsley to the mixture and season to taste with salt and pepper. Add 1 tablespoon of the beaten egg to bind the mixture together. Chill in the refrigerator for at least 1 hour.

3 Shape the chilled mixture with your hands into 4 large burgers. First, coat the burgers with seasoned flour, then brush them with the remaining beaten egg, allowing any excess to drip back into the bowl. Finally, coat them evenly in the breadcrumbs, pressing the crumbs on with your hands, if necessary.

4 Heat a little of the oil in a frying pan and fry the burgers for 2–3 minutes on each side until golden, adding more oil if necessary. Drain on absorbent kitchen paper and serve hot in baps, if using, with chips, mixed salad and chutney.

Ingredients

MAKES 8

450 g/1 lb potatoes, peeled and cut into chunks
50 g/2 oz butter
2 tbsp milk
400 g can tuna in oil
1 spring onion, trimmed and finely chopped
1 tbsp freshly chopped parsley
salt and freshly ground black pepper
2 medium eggs, beaten
2 tbsp seasoned plain flour
125 g/4 oz fresh white breadcrumbs
4 tbsp vegetable oil
4 sesame seed baps (optional)

To serve:
fat chips
mixed salad
tomato chutney

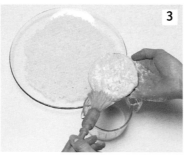

Bombay Tuna Patties

1 Lightly oil a nonstick frying pan with about 2 teaspoons of oil and gently cook the tuna fish for 2–3 minutes on each side, or until just cooked. Remove and leave until cool enough to handle. Chop roughly and place in a mixing bowl.

2 Cook the potatoes in a saucepan of boiling water for 12–15 minutes, or until tender. Drain and mash into a chunky rather than smooth consistency.

3 Add to the tuna together with the turmeric and mix lightly together. Heat the remaining oil in the frying pan, add the seeds and fry for 30 seconds, or until they pop. Add the remaining spices and continue to fry gently for 2 minutes, stirring constantly. Remove and stir into the tuna mixture and mix well.

4 Using damp hands, shape the tuna mixture into 8–12 small rounds and place on a plate. Blend the cornflour with the water to form a coating batter. Place the breadcrumbs on a plate.

5 Heat the oil for deep-frying in a deep, large saucepan or wok to a temperature of 180°C/350°F. Dip the tuna patties into the cornflour and then in the breadcrumbs. Deep-fry, in batches, for 2–3 minutes, or until golden and crisp. Drain on absorbent kitchen paper. Repeat until all the patties are cooked. Serve with salad, tomato chutney and/or Raita.

Ingredients   SERVES 4-6

2 tbsp vegetable oil, plus extra for deep-frying
300 g/10 oz fresh tuna steaks
225 g/8 oz potatoes, peeled and cut into small chunks
1/2 tsp turmeric
1 tsp cumin seeds
1 tsp fenugreek seeds
1 tsp ground coriander
1 tsp garam masala
few curry leaves
1 tsp ginger purée
1/2–1 tsp chilli powder, or to taste
75 g/3 oz cornflour
50–85 ml/2–3 fl oz water
75 g/3 oz dried breadcrumbs

To serve:

tomato chutney, raita or fresh salad

Helpful Hint

Fresh breadcrumbs are better than shop-bought. Dry fresh breadcrumbs in a hot oven until they separate.

Salmon Fish Cakes

1 Place the salmon in a shallow frying pan and cover with water. Season to taste with salt and pepper and simmer for 8–10 minutes until the fish is cooked. Drain and flake into a bowl.

2 Boil the potatoes in lightly salted water until soft, then drain. Mash with the butter and milk until smooth. Add the potato to the bowl of fish and stir in the tomatoes and half the parsley. Adjust the seasoning to taste. Chill the mixture in the refrigerator for at least 2 hours to firm up.

3 Mix the breadcrumbs with the grated cheese and the remaining parsley. When the fish mixture is firm, form into 8 flat cakes. First, lightly coat the fish cakes in the flour, then dip into the beaten egg, allowing any excess to drip back into the bowl. Finally, press into the breadcrumb mixture until well coated.

4 Heat a little of the oil in a frying pan and fry the fish cakes in batches for 2–3 minutes on each side until golden and crisp, adding more oil if necessary. Serve with raita garnished with sprigs of mint.

Ingredients   SERVES 4

450 g/1 lb salmon fillet, skinned
salt and freshly ground black pepper
450 g/1 lb potatoes, peeled and
    cut into chunks
25 g/1 oz butter
1 tbsp milk
2 medium tomatoes, skinned,
    deseeded and chopped
2 tbsp freshly chopped parsley
75 g/3 oz wholemeal breadcrumbs
25 g/1 oz Cheddar cheese, grated
2 tbsp plain flour
2 medium eggs, beaten
3–4 tbsp vegetable oil

To serve:
ready-made raita
sprigs of fresh mint

Helpful Hint
To remove the tomatoes' skins, pierce each with the tip of a sharp knife, plunge into boiling water and leave for up to 1 minute. Drain, then rinse in cold water – the skins should peel off easily.

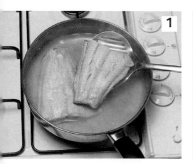

Potato Pancakes with Smoked Salmon

1 Cook the potatoes in a saucepan of lightly salted boiling water for 15–20 minutes, or until tender. Drain thoroughly, then mash until free of lumps. Beat in the whole egg and egg yolk, together with the butter. Beat until smooth and creamy. Slowly beat in the flour and cream, then season to taste with salt and pepper. Stir in the chopped parsley.

2 Beat the crème fraîche and horseradish sauce together in a small bowl, cover with clingfilm and reserve.

3 Heat a lightly oiled, heavy-based frying pan over a medium-high heat. Place a few spoonfuls of the potato mixture in the hot pan and cook for 4–5 minutes, or until cooked and golden, turning halfway through the cooking time. Remove from the pan, drain on absorbent kitchen paper and keep warm. Repeat with the remaining mixture.

4 Arrange the pancakes on individual serving plates. Place the smoked salmon on the pancakes and spoon over a little of the horseradish sauce. Serve with salad and the remaining horseradish sauce and garnish with lemon slices and chives.

Ingredients   SERVES 4

450 g/1 lb floury potatoes, peeled
    and quartered
salt and freshly ground black pepper
1 large egg
1 large egg yolk
25 g/1 oz butter
25 g/1 oz plain flour
150 ml/¼ pint double cream
2 tbsp freshly chopped parsley
5 tbsp crème fraîche
1 tbsp horseradish sauce
225 g/8 oz smoked salmon, sliced
salad leaves, to serve

To garnish:
lemon slices
snipped chives

Tasty Tip
Commercially-made sauces vary in heat, so it is best to add a little at a time to the crème fraîche and taste until you have the desired flavour.

Salmon with Herbed Potatoes

1 Preheat the oven to 190°C/375°F/Gas Mark 5, about 10 minutes before required. Parboil the potatoes in lightly salted boiling water for 5–8 minutes until they are barely tender. Drain and reserve.

2 Cut out 4 pieces of baking parchment paper, measuring 20.5 cm/8 inches square, and place on the work surface. Arrange the parboiled potatoes on top. Wipe the salmon steaks and place on top of the potatoes.

3 Place the carrot strips in a bowl with the asparagus spears, sugar snaps and grated lemon rind and juice. Season to taste with salt and pepper. Toss lightly together.

4 Divide the vegetables evenly between the salmon. Dot the top of each parcel with butter and add a sprig of parsley.

5 To wrap a parcel, lift up 2 opposite sides of the paper and fold the edges together. Twist the paper at the other 2 ends to seal the parcel well. Repeat with the remaining parcels.

6 Place the parcels on a baking tray and bake in the preheated oven for 15 minutes. Place an unopened parcel on each plate and open just before eating.

Ingredients SERVES 4

450 g/1 lb baby new potatoes
salt and freshly ground black pepper
4 salmon steaks, each weighing about
175 g/6 oz
1 carrot, peeled and cut into fine strips
175 g/6 oz asparagus spears, trimmed
175 g/6 oz sugar snap peas, trimmed
finely grated rind and juice of 1 lemon
25 g/1 oz butter
4 large sprigs of fresh parsley

Helpful Hint

Cooking fish en papillote is an excellent way of keeping in all the juices, flavour and aroma of the fish and vegetables. Your guests will also enjoy the anticipation of opening these surprise packages. Do let the parcels stand for a few minutes before serving as the steam can be burning hot when opened.

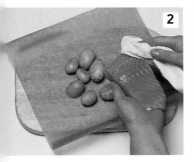

Smoked Salmon Quiche

1 Preheat the oven to 200°C/400°F/Gas Mark 6. Blend the flour, butter and white vegetable fat or lard together until it resembles fine breadcrumbs. Blend again, adding sufficient water to make a firm but pliable dough. Use the dough to line a 23 cm/9 inch flan dish or tin, then chill the pastry case in the refrigerator for 30 minutes. Bake blind with baking beans for 10 minutes.

2 Heat the oil in a small frying pan, add the diced potato and cook for 3–4 minutes until lightly browned. Reduce the heat and cook for 2–3 minutes, or until tender. Leave to cool.

3 Scatter the grated cheese evenly over the base of the pastry case, then arrange the cooled potato on top. Add the smoked salmon in an even layer.

4 Beat the eggs with the cream and season to taste with salt and pepper. Whisk in the parsley and pour the mixture carefully into the dish.

5 Reduce the oven to 180°C/350°F/Gas Mark 4 and bake for about 30–40 minutes, or until the filling is set and golden. Serve hot or cold with a mixed salad and baby new potatoes.

Ingredients　　　SERVES 6

225 g/8 oz plain flour
50 g/2 oz butter
50 g/2 oz white vegetable fat or lard
2 tsp sunflower oil
225 g/8 oz potato, peeled and diced
125 g/4 oz Gruyère cheese, grated
75 g/3 oz smoked salmon trimmings
5 medium eggs, beaten
300 ml/½ pint single cream
salt and freshly ground black pepper
1 tbsp freshly chopped flat-leaf parsley

To serve:
mixed salad
baby new potatoes

Tasty Tip
Using lard or white vegetable fat with the butter makes a deliciously short-textured pastry, but you can use all butter if you prefer a richer flavour and colour. Do not be tempted to leave out the chilling time for the pastry case. This allows the pastry to rest and helps to minimise shrinkage during baking.

Battered Cod & Chunky Chips

1 Dissolve the yeast with a little of the beer in a jug and mix to a paste. Pour in the remaining beer, whisking all the time until smooth. Place the flour and salt in a bowl and gradually pour in the beer mixture, whisking continuously to make a thick, smooth batter. Cover the bowl and allow the batter to stand at room temperature for 1 hour.

2 Peel the potatoes and cut into thick slices. Cut each slice lengthways to make chunky chips. Place them in a nonstick frying pan and heat, shaking the pan until all the moisture has evaporated. Turn them onto absorbent kitchen paper to dry off.

3 Heat the oil to 180°C/350°F, then fry the chips a few at a time for 4–5 minutes until crisp and golden. Drain on absorbent kitchen paper and keep warm.

4 Pat the cod fillets dry, then coat in the flour. Dip the floured fillets into the reserved batter. Fry for 2–3 minutes until cooked and crisp, then drain. Garnish with lemon wedges and parsley and serve immediately with the chips, tomato ketchup and vinegar.

Ingredients   SERVES 4

15 g/½ oz fresh yeast
300 ml/½ pint beer
225 g/8 oz plain flour
1 tsp salt
700 g/1½ lb potatoes
450 ml/¾ pint groundnut oil
4 cod fillets, about 225 g/8 oz each, skinned and boned
2 tbsp seasoned plain flour

To garnish:

lemon wedges
sprigs of flat-leaf parsley

To serve:

tomato ketchup
vinegar

Helpful Hint

When mixed with warm liquid, yeast produces gases which lighten this batter. When buying fresh yeast, check that it is moist and creamy-coloured and has a strong yeasty smell.

Spanish Omelette with Smoked Cod

1 Heat the oil in a large, nonstick heavy-based frying pan, add the potatoes, onions and garlic and cook gently for 10–15 minutes until golden brown, then add the red pepper and cook for 3 minutes.

2 Meanwhile, place the fish in a shallow frying pan and cover with water. Season to taste with salt and pepper and poach gently for 10 minutes. Drain and flake the fish into a bowl, toss in the melted butter and cream, adjust the seasoning and reserve.

3 When the vegetables are cooked, drain off any excess oil and stir in the beaten egg with the chopped parsley. Pour the fish mixture over the top and cook gently for 5 minutes, or until the eggs become firm.

4 Sprinkle the grated cheese over the top and place the pan under a preheated hot grill. Cook for 2–3 minutes until the cheese is golden and bubbling. Carefully slide the omelette onto a large plate and serve immediately with plenty of bread and salad.

Ingredients   SERVES 3–4

3 tbsp sunflower oil
350 g/12 oz potatoes, peeled and cut into 1 cm/½ inch cubes
2 medium onions, peeled and cut into wedges
2–4 large garlic cloves, peeled and thinly sliced
1 large red pepper, deseeded, quartered and thinly sliced
125 g/4 oz smoked cod
salt and freshly ground black pepper
25 g/1 oz butter, melted
1 tbsp double cream
6 medium eggs, beaten
2 tbsp freshly chopped flat-leaf parsley
50 g/2 oz mature Cheddar cheese, grated

To serve:
crusty bread
tossed green salad

Helpful Hint
Finishing the dish under the grill gives it a delicious golden look.

Chunky Halibut Casserole

1 Melt the butter or margarine in a large saucepan, add the onions and pepper and cook for 5 minutes, or until softened.

2 Cut the peeled potatoes into 2.5 cm/1 inch dice, rinse lightly and shake dry, then add them to the onions and pepper in the saucepan. Add the courgettes and cook, stirring frequently, for a further 2–3 minutes.

3 Sprinkle the flour, paprika and vegetable oil into the saucepan and cook, stirring continuously, for 1 minute. Pour in 150 ml/$^{1}/_{4}$ pint of the wine, with all the stock and the chopped tomatoes, and bring to the boil.

4 Add the basil to the casserole, season to taste with salt and pepper and cover. Simmer for 15 minutes, then add the halibut and the remaining wine and simmer very gently for a further 5–7 minutes, or until the fish and vegetables are just tender. Garnish with basil sprigs and serve immediately with freshly cooked rice.

Ingredients   SERVES 6

50 g/2 oz butter or margarine
2 large onions, peeled and
    sliced into rings
1 red pepper, deseeded and
    roughly chopped
450 g/1 lb potatoes, peeled
450 g/1 lb courgettes, trimmed and
    thickly sliced
2 tbsp plain flour
1 tbsp paprika
2 tsp vegetable oil
300 ml/$^{1}/_{2}$ pint white wine
150 ml/$^{1}/_{4}$ pint fish stock
400 g can chopped tomatoes
2 tbsp freshly chopped basil
salt and freshly ground black pepper
450 g/1 lb halibut fillet, skinned and
    cut into 2.5 cm/1 inch cubes
sprigs of fresh basil, to garnish
freshly cooked rice, to serve

Supreme Baked Potatoes

1 Preheat the oven to 200°C/400°F/Gas Mark 6. Scrub the potatoes and prick all over with a fork, or thread 2 potatoes onto 2 long metal skewers. Place the potatoes in the preheated oven for 1–1¹/₂ hours, or until soft to the touch.

2 Before the potatoes are finished cooking, heat the oil in a frying pan and cook the carrot and celery for 2 minutes. Cover the pan tightly and continue to cook for another 5 minutes, or until the vegetables are tender. Reserve.

3 Allow the potatoes to cool a little, then cut in half. Scoop out the cooked potato and turn into a bowl, leaving a reasonably firm potato shell. Mash the cooked potato flesh, then mix in the butter and mash until the butter has melted.

4 Add the cooked vegetables to the bowl of mashed potato and mix well. Fold in the crab meat and the spring onions, then season to taste with salt and pepper.

5 Pile the mixture back into the potato shells and press in firmly. Sprinkle the grated cheese over the top and return the potato halves to the oven for 12–15 minutes until hot, golden and bubbling. Serve immediately with a tomato salad.

Ingredients   SERVES 4

4 large baking potatoes
40 g/1¹/₂ oz butter
1 tbsp sunflower oil
1 carrot, peeled and chopped
2 celery sticks, trimmed and finely
   chopped
200 g can white crab meat
2 spring onions, trimmed and
   finely chopped
salt and freshly ground black pepper
50 g/2 oz Cheddar cheese, grated
tomato salad, to serve

Tasty Tip

Threading the potatoes onto metal skewers helps them to cook more evenly and quickly as heat is transferred via the metal to the centres of the potatoes during cooking. To give the skins a crunchier finish, rub them with a little oil and lightly sprinkle with salt before baking.

Smoked Mackerel & Potato Salad

1 Place the mustard powder and egg yolk in a small bowl with salt and pepper and whisk until blended. Add the oil, drop by drop, into the egg mixture, whisking continuously. When the mayonnaise is thick, add the lemon juice, drop by drop, until a smooth, glossy consistency is formed. Reserve.

2 Cook the potatoes in boiling salted water until tender, then drain. Cool slightly, then cut into halves or quarters, depending on size. Return to the saucepan and toss in the butter.

3 Remove the skin from the mackerel fillets and flake into pieces. Add to the potatoes in the saucepan, together with the celery.

4 Blend 4 tablespoons of the mayonnaise with the horseradish and crème fraîche. Season to taste with salt and pepper, then add to the potato and mackerel mixture and stir lightly.

5 Arrange the lettuce and tomatoes on 4 serving plates. Pile the smoked mackerel mixture on top of the lettuce, grind over a little pepper and serve with the remaining mayonnaise.

Ingredients   SERVES 4

$^1/_2$ tsp dry mustard powder
1 large egg yolk
salt and freshly ground black pepper
150 ml/$^1/_4$ pint sunflower oil
1–2 tbsp lemon juice
450 g/1 lb baby new potatoes
25 g/1 oz butter
350 g/12 oz smoked mackerel fillets
4 celery sticks, trimmed and finely
    chopped
3 tbsp creamed horseradish
150 ml/$^1/_4$ pint crème fraîche
1 little gem lettuce, rinsed and
    roughly torn
8 cherry tomatoes, halved

Helpful Hint

When making mayonnaise, ensure that the ingredients are at room temperature, or it may curdle. For speed, it can be made in a food processor: briefly blend the mustard, egg yolk, seasoning and lemon juice, then, with the motor running, slowly pour in the oil.

Traditional Fish Pie

1 Preheat the oven to 200°C/400°F/Gas Mark 6, about 15 minutes before cooking. Place the fish in a shallow frying pan, pour over 300 ml/^{1}/$_2$ pint of the milk and add the onion. Season to taste with salt and pepper. Bring to the boil and simmer for 8–10 minutes until the fish is cooked. Remove the fish with a slotted spoon and place in a 1.4 litre/2^1/$_2$ pint baking dish. Strain the cooking liquid and reserve.

2 Boil the potatoes until soft, then mash with 40 g/1^1/$_2$ oz of the butter and 2–3 tablespoons of the remaining milk. Reserve.

3 Arrange the prawns and sliced eggs on top of the fish, then scatter over the sweetcorn and sprinkle with the parsley.

4 Melt the remaining butter in a saucepan, stir in the flour and cook gently for 1 minute, stirring. Whisk in the reserved cooking liquid and remaining milk. Cook for 2 minutes, or until thickened, then pour over the fish mixture and cool slightly.

5 Spread the mashed potato over the top of the pie and sprinkle over the grated cheese. Bake in the preheated oven for 30 minutes until golden. Serve immediately.

Ingredients   SERVES 4

450 g/1 lb cod or coley fillets, skinned
450 ml/^{3}/$_4$ pint milk
1 small onion, peeled and quartered
salt and freshly ground black pepper
900 g/2 lb potatoes, peeled and cut into chunks
100 g/3^1/$_2$ oz butter
125 g/4 oz large prawns
2 large eggs, hard-boiled and quartered
198 g can sweetcorn, drained
2 tbsp freshly chopped parsley
3 tbsp plain flour
50 g/2 oz Cheddar cheese, grated

Tasty Tip

Any variety of white fish may be used in this delicious dish, including haddock, hake, ling, pollack and whiting. You could also used smoked fish, such as smoked cod or haddock, for a change. After simmering in milk, carefully check and remove any bones from the cooked fish.

Fish Crumble

1 Preheat the oven to 200°C/400°F/Gas Mark 6, 15 minutes before cooking. Oil a 1.4 litre/2¹/₂ pint pie dish. Place the fish in a saucepan with the milk, salt and pepper. Bring to the boil, cover and simmer for 8–10 minutes until the fish is cooked. Remove with a slotted spoon, reserving the cooking liquid. Flake the fish into the prepared dish.

2 Heat the oil and 1 tablespoon of the butter or margarine in a small frying pan and gently fry the onion, leeks, carrot and potatoes for 1–2 minutes. Cover tightly and cook over a gentle heat for a further 10 minutes until softened. Spoon the vegetables over the fish.

3 Melt the remaining butter or margarine in a saucepan, add the flour and cook for 1 minute, stirring. Whisk in the reserved cooking liquid and the stock. Cook until thickened, then stir in the cream. Remove from the heat and stir in the dill. Pour over the fish.

4 To make the crumble, rub the butter or margarine into the flour until it resembles breadcrumbs, then stir in the cheese and cayenne pepper. Sprinkle over the dish and bake in the preheated oven for 20 minutes until piping hot. Serve with runner beans.

Ingredients   SERVES 6

450 g/1 lb whiting or halibut fillets
300 ml/¹/₂ pint milk
salt and freshly ground black pepper
1 tbsp sunflower oil
75 g/3 oz butter or margarine
1 medium onion, peeled and
    finely chopped
2 leeks, trimmed and sliced
1 medium carrot, peeled and cut
    into small dice
2 medium potatoes, peeled and
    cut into small pieces
175 g/6 oz plain flour
300 ml/¹/₂ pint fish or vegetable stock
2 tbsp whipping cream
1 tsp freshly chopped dill
runner beans, to serve

For the crumble topping:
75 g/3 oz butter or margarine
175 g/6 oz plain flour
75 g/3 oz Parmesan cheese, grated
³/₄ tsp cayenne pepper

Smoked Fish Pie

1 For the sauce, heat the butter in a large saucepan and, when melted, add the flour and mustard powder. Stir until smooth and cook over a very low heat for 2 minutes without colouring. Slowly beat in the milk until smooth. Simmer gently for 2 minutes, then stir in the cheese until smooth. Remove from the heat and put some clingfilm over the surface of the sauce to prevent a skin forming. Set aside.

2 Meanwhile, for the topping, boil the potatoes in salted water for 15 minutes. Drain well and set aside until cool enough to handle.

3 Heat the olive oil in a clean pan and add the onion. Cook for 5 minutes until softened. Add the leek, carrot, celery and mushrooms and cook for a further 10 minutes until the vegetables have softened. Stir in the lemon rind and cook briefly. Add the softened vegetables with the fish, prawns, parsley and dill to the sauce. Season with salt and pepper and transfer to a greased 1.75 litre/3 pint baking dish.

4 Peel the cooled potatoes and grate coarsely. Mix with the melted butter. Cover the filling with the grated potato and sprinkle with the grated Gruyère cheese. Cover loosely with foil and bake in a preheated oven at 200˚C/400˚F/Gas Mark 6 for 30 minutes. Remove the foil and bake for a further 30 minutes until the topping is tender and golden and the filling is bubbling. Serve immediately with your favourite selection of vegetables.

Ingredients SERVES 6

2 tbsp olive oil
1 onion, finely chopped
1 leek, thinly sliced
1 carrot, diced
1 celery stick, diced
125 g/4 oz button mushrooms
grated rind of 1 lemon
375 g/12 oz skinless, boneless smoked cod or haddock fillet, cubed
375 g/12 oz skinless, boneless white fish such as haddock, hake or monkfish, cubed
225 g/8 oz cooked peeled prawns
2 tbsp fresh parsley, chopped
1 tbsp fresh dill, chopped

For the sauce:

50 g/2 oz butter; 40 g/1^3/$_4$ oz plain flour; 1 tsp mustard powder; 600 ml/1 pint milk; 80 g/3 oz Gruyère cheese, grated

For the topping:

750 g/1^1/$_2$ lb potatoes, unpeeled; 50 g/ 2 oz butter, melted; 25 g/1 oz Gruyère cheese, grated; salt and black pepper

Potato Boulangere with Sea Bass

1 Preheat the oven to 200°C/400°F/Gas Mark 6. Lightly grease a shallow 1.4 litre/2½ pint baking dish with oil or butter. Layer the potato slices and onions alternately in the prepared dish, seasoning each layer with salt and pepper.

2 Pour the stock over the top, then cut 50 g/2 oz of the butter or margarine into small pieces and dot over the top layer. Bake in the preheated oven for 50–60 minutes. Do not cover the dish at this stage.

3 Lightly rinse the sea bass fillets and pat dry on absorbent kitchen paper. Cook on a griddle or heat the remaining butter or margarine in a frying pan and shallow fry the fish fillets for 3–4 minutes per side, flesh side first. Remove from the pan with a slotted spatula and drain on absorbent kitchen paper.

4 Remove the partly cooked potato and onion mixture from the oven and place the fish on the top. Cover with foil and return to the oven for 10 minutes until heated through. Garnish with sprigs of parsley and serve immediately.

Ingredients   SERVES 2

450 g/1 lb potatoes, peeled and
    thinly sliced
1 large onion, peeled and thinly sliced
salt and freshly ground black pepper
300 ml/½ pint fish or vegetable stock
75 g/3 oz butter or margarine
350 g/12 oz sea bass fillets
sprigs of fresh flat-leaf parsley,
    to garnish

Food Fact
Sea bass is similar to salmon in appearance, but a much darker grey colour. Cook it gently and handle it with care, as the flesh is soft and delicate.

Scallop & Potato Gratin

1 Preheat the oven to 220°C/425°F/Gas Mark 7. Clean 4 scallop shells to use as serving dishes and reserve. Place the scallops in a small saucepan with the wine, 150 ml/¼ pint water and salt and pepper. Cover and simmer very gently for 5 minutes, or until just tender. Remove with a slotted spoon and cut each scallop into 3 pieces. Reserve the cooking juices.

2 Melt 25 g/1 oz of the butter in a saucepan, stir in the flour and cook for 1 minute, stirring, then gradually whisk in the reserved cooking juices. Simmer, stirring, for 3–4 minutes until the sauce has thickened. Season to taste with salt and pepper. Remove from the heat and stir in the cream and 25 g/1 oz of the grated cheese. Fold in the scallops.

3 Boil the potatoes in lightly salted water until tender, then mash with the remaining butter and milk. Spoon or pipe the mashed potato around the edges of the cleaned scallop shells.

4 Divide the scallop mixture between the 4 shells, placing the mixture neatly in the centre. Sprinkle with the remaining grated cheese and bake in the preheated oven for about 10–15 minutes until golden brown and bubbling. Serve immediately.

Ingredients   SERVES 4

8 fresh scallops in their shells,
  cleaned
4 tbsp white wine
salt and freshly ground black pepper
50 g/2 oz butter
3 tbsp plain flour
2 tbsp single cream
50 g/2 oz Cheddar cheese, grated
450 g/1 lb potatoes, peeled and
  cut into chunks
1 tbsp milk

Helpful Hint

You can ask your fishmonger to open and clean the scallops if you plan to cook them on the same day. Alternatively, buy scallops live and keep in the refrigerator for up to 24 hours. The simplest and safest way to open scallops is to place them flat side up on a baking sheet and put in a hot oven for a few minutes. Prise open the 2 shells and remove the white scallop meat and the bright orange coral.

Meat & Poultry

If you fancy ramping up your ordinary meat and two veg, take your pick from this selection. Shepherd's Pie and Lancashire Hotpot are essentials on any weekly menu, and how about accompanying your Grilled Steaks with Saffron Potatoes & Roast Tomatoes? Chicken Pie with Sweet Potato Topping is scrumptious and light, while Chicken Marengo Casserole and Lamb & Date Tagine will add spice to your suppertime.

Roast Leg of Lamb & Boulangere Potatoes

1 Preheat the oven to 230°C/450°F/Gas Mark 8. Finely slice the potatoes – a mandolin is the best tool for this. Layer the potatoes with the onion in a large roasting tin, seasoning each layer with salt and pepper. Drizzle about 1 tablespoon of the olive oil over the potatoes and add the butter in small pieces. Pour in the lamb stock and milk. Set aside.

2 Make small incisions all over the lamb with the point of a small, sharp knife. Into each incision, insert a small piece of rosemary, a sliver of garlic and a piece of anchovy fillet.

3 Drizzle the leg of lamb and its flavourings with the rest of the olive oil and season well. Place the meat directly onto a shelf in the preheated oven. Position the roasting tin of potatoes directly underneath to catch the juices during cooking. Roast for 15 minutes per 500 g/1 lb 2 oz (about 1 hour for a joint this size), reducing the oven temperature after 20 minutes to 200°C/400°F/Gas Mark 6.

4 When the lamb is cooked, remove from the oven and allow to rest for 10 minutes before carving. Meanwhile, increase the oven heat and cook the potatoes for a further 10–15 minutes to crisp up. Garnish with fresh rosemary sprigs and serve immediately with the lamb.

Ingredients   SERVES 6

1.1 kg/2¹/₂ lb potatoes, peeled
1 large onion, peeled and finely sliced
salt and freshly ground black pepper
2 tbsp olive oil
50 g/2 oz butter
200 ml/7 fl oz lamb stock
100 ml/3¹/₂ fl oz milk
2 kg/4¹/₂ lb leg of lamb
2–3 sprigs of fresh rosemary
6 large garlic cloves, peeled and
    finely sliced
6 anchovy fillets, drained
extra sprigs of fresh rosemary, to
    garnish

Food Fact

Leg of lamb is one of the prime roasting joints and is known by its French name *gigot* in Scotland. It may weigh between 1.8–2.7 kg/4–6 lb, so ask for a small joint for this dish. Although home-produced lamb is at its best in the spring, there is a good supply all year round of imported New Zealand lamb.

Lancashire Hotpot

1 Preheat the oven to 170°C/325°F/Gas Mark 3. Trim any excess fat from the lamb cutlets. Heat the oil in a frying pan and brown the cutlets, in batches, for 3–4 minutes. Remove with a slotted spoon and reserve. Add the onions to the frying pan and cook for 6–8 minutes until softened and just beginning to colour, then remove and reserve.

2 Stir in the flour and cook for a few seconds, then gradually pour in the stock, stirring well, and bring to the boil. Remove from the heat.

3 Spread the base of a large casserole with half the potato slices. Top with half the onions and season well with salt and pepper. Arrange the browned meat in a layer. Season again and add the remaining onions, bay leaf and thyme. Pour in the remaining liquid from the onions and top with the remaining potatoes so that they overlap in a single layer. Brush the potatoes with the melted butter and season again.

4 Cover the saucepan and cook in the preheated oven for 2 hours, uncovering for the last 30 minutes to allow the potatoes to brown. Garnish with chopped herbs and serve immediately with green beans.

Ingredients   SERVES 4

1 kg/2¹/₄ lb middle end neck of lamb, divided into cutlets
2 tbsp vegetable oil
2 large onions, peeled and sliced
2 tsp plain flour
150 ml/¹/₄ pint vegetable or lamb stock
700 g/1¹/₂ lb waxy potatoes, peeled and thickly sliced
salt and freshly ground black pepper
1 bay leaf
2 sprigs of fresh thyme
1 tbsp melted butter
2 tbsp freshly chopped herbs, to garnish
freshly cooked green beans, to serve

Food Fact

The name of this classic dish derives from the past tradition of wrapping it in blankets after cooking to keep it warm until lunchtime. There are dozens of versions all claiming to be authentic. Some include lambs' kidneys to enrich the gravy but, whatever the ingredients, it is important to season well and to cook it slowly, so the lamb is meltingly tender.

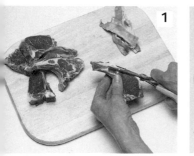

Shepherd's Pie

1 Preheat the oven to 200°C/400°F/Gas Mark 6, about 15 minutes before cooking. Heat the oil in a large saucepan and add the onion, carrot and celery. Cook over a medium heat for 8–10 minutes until softened and starting to brown.

2 Add the thyme and cook briefly, then add the cooked lamb, wine, stock and tomato purée. Season to taste with salt and pepper and simmer gently for 25–30 minutes until reduced and thickened. Remove from the heat to cool slightly and season again.

3 Meanwhile, boil the potatoes in plenty of salted water for 12–15 minutes until tender. Drain and return to the saucepan over a low heat to dry out. Remove from the heat and add the butter, milk and parsley. Mash until creamy, adding a little more milk if necessary. Adjust the seasoning.

4 Transfer the lamb mixture to a shallow ovenproof dish. Spoon the mash over the filling and spread evenly to cover completely. Fork the surface, place on a baking sheet, then cook in the preheated oven for 25–30 minutes until the potato topping is browned and the filling is piping hot. Garnish and serve.

Ingredients   SERVES 4

2 tbsp vegetable or olive oil
1 onion, peeled and finely chopped
1 carrot, peeled and finely chopped
1 celery stick, trimmed and finely
  chopped
1 tbsp sprigs of fresh thyme
450 g/1 lb leftover roast lamb, finely
  chopped
150 ml/¹/₄ pint red wine
150 ml/¹/₄ pint lamb or vegetable
  stock or leftover gravy
2 tbsp tomato purée
salt and freshly ground black pepper
700 g/1¹/₂ lb potatoes, peeled and
  cut into chunks
25 g/1 oz butter
6 tbsp milk
1 tbsp freshly chopped parsley
fresh herbs, to garnish

Tasty Tip
You can make this with fresh minced lamb if preferred. Simply brown 450 g/ 1 lb lean mince in a nonstick frying pan, then follow the recipe as before.

Lamb & Potato Moussaka

1 Preheat the oven to 200°C/400°F/Gas Mark 6, about 15 minutes before required. Trim the lamb, discarding any fat, then cut into fine dice and reserve. Thinly slice the potatoes and rinse thoroughly in cold water, then pat dry with a clean tea towel.

2 Melt 50 g/2 oz of the butter in a frying pan and fry the potatoes, in batches, until crisp and golden. Using a slotted spoon, remove from the pan and reserve. Use a third of the potatoes to line the base of an ovenproof dish.

3 Add the onion and garlic to the butter remaining in the pan and cook for 5 minutes. Add the lamb and fry for 1 minute. Blend the tomato purée with 3 tablespoons of water and stir into the pan with the parsley and salt and pepper. Spoon over the layer of potatoes, then top with the remaining potato slices.

4 Heat the oil and the remaining butter in the pan and brown the aubergine slices for 5–6 minutes. Arrange the tomatoes on top of the potatoes, then the aubergines on top of the tomatoes. Beat the eggs with the yogurt and Parmesan cheese and pour over the aubergine and tomatoes. Bake in the preheated oven for 25 minutes, or until golden and piping hot. Serve.

Ingredients   SERVES 4

700 g/1½ lb cooked roast lamb
700 g/1½ lb potatoes, peeled
125 g/4 oz butter
1 large onion, peeled and chopped
2–4 garlic cloves, peeled and crushed
3 tbsp tomato purée
1 tbsp freshly chopped parsley
salt and freshly ground black pepper
3–4 tbsp olive oil
2 medium aubergines, trimmed and sliced
4 medium tomatoes, sliced
2 medium eggs
300 ml/½ pint Greek yogurt
2–3 tbsp Parmesan cheese, grated

Handy Hint

It is worth salting the aubergines to ensure that any bitterness is removed. Layer the slices in a colander, sprinkling a little salt between the layers. Leave for 20 minutes, then rinse under cold running water and pat dry on absorbent kitchen paper. Salting helps the aubergines to absorb less oil when frying.

Slow-roasted Lamb

1 Preheat the oven to 190°C/375°F/Gas Mark 5. Wipe the lamb with absorbent kitchen paper and make small slits over the lamb. Reserve.

2 Heat the oil in a frying pan, add the seeds and fry for 30 seconds, stirring. Add the remaining spices, including the 2 garlic cloves and green chillies, and cook for 5 minutes. Remove and use half to spread over the lamb.

3 Cut the potatoes into bite-size chunks and the onions into wedges. Cut the garlic in half. Place in a roasting tin and cover with the remaining spice paste, then place the lamb on top.

4 Cook in the preheated oven for 1¼–1½ hours, or until the lamb and potatoes are cooked. Turn the potatoes over occasionally during cooking. Serve the lamb with the potatoes and freshly cooked vegetables.

Ingredients   SERVES 6

1 leg of lamb, about 1.5 kg/3 lb
    in weight
2 tbsp vegetable oil
1 tsp fennel seeds
1 tsp cumin seeds
1 tsp ground coriander
1 tsp turmeric
2 garlic cloves, peeled and crushed
2 green chillies, deseeded and
    chopped
freshly cooked vegetables, to serve

For the potatoes:

550 g/1¼ lb potatoes, peeled
2 onions, peeled
4 garlic cloves, peeled

Tasty Tip

Roasted assorted peppers, aubergine and courgettes would be perfect to serve with this dish. Trim and dice the vegetables, pour over 2 tablespoons of oil and roast with the lamb for the last 35 minutes of cooking time.

Roasted Lamb with Rosemary & Garlic

1 Preheat the oven to 200°C/400°F/Gas Mark 6, 15 minutes before roasting. Wipe the leg of lamb with a clean damp cloth, then place the lamb in a large roasting tin. With a sharp knife, make small, deep incisions into the meat. Cut 2–3 garlic cloves into small slivers, then insert with a few small sprigs of rosemary into the lamb. Season to taste with salt and pepper and cover the lamb with the slices of pancetta.

2 Drizzle over 1 tablespoon of the olive oil and lay a few more rosemary sprigs across the lamb. Roast in the preheated oven for 30 minutes, then pour over the vinegar.

3 Peel the potatoes and cut into large dice. Peel the onion and cut into thick wedges, then thickly slice the remaining garlic. Arrange around the lamb. Pour the remaining olive oil over the potatoes, then reduce the oven temperature to 180°C/350°F/Gas Mark 4 and roast for a further 1 hour, or until the lamb is tender. Garnish with sprigs of fresh rosemary and serve immediately with the roast potatoes and ratatouille.

Ingredients   SERVES 6

1.6 kg/3^1/$_2$ lb leg of lamb
8 garlic cloves, peeled
few sprigs of fresh rosemary
salt and freshly ground black pepper
4 slices pancetta
4 tbsp olive oil
4 tbsp red wine vinegar
900 g/2 lb potatoes
1 large onion
sprigs of fresh rosemary, to garnish
freshly cooked ratatouille, to serve

Helpful Hint

If you are unable to get a leg of lamb weighing exactly 1.6 kg/3^1/$_2$ lb, calculate the cooking time as follows: 20 minutes per 450 g/1 lb plus 30 minutes for rare, 25 minutes per 450 g/1 lb plus 30 minutes for medium and 30 minutes per 450 g/1 lb plus 30 minutes for well done.

Lamb & Potato Curry

1 Discard any fat or gristle from the lamb, then cut into thin strips and reserve.

2 Heat the oil in a deep frying pan, add the onions, garlic and celery and fry for 5 minutes, or until softened. Add the ginger, chillies, curry leaves and spices and continue to fry for a further 3 minutes, stirring constantly. Add the lamb and cook for 5 minutes, or until coated in the spices.

3 Blend the tomato purée with the water, then stir into the pan together with the coconut milk and chopped tomatoes.

4 Cut the potatoes into small chunks and add to the pan with the carrots. Bring to the boil, then reduce the heat, cover and simmer for 25–30 minutes, or until the lamb and vegetables are tender. Serve with freshly cooked rice.

Ingredients SERVES 4

450 g/1 lb lean lamb, such as leg steaks
2 tbsp vegetable oil
2 onions, peeled and cut into wedges
2–3 garlic cloves, peeled and sliced
2 celery sticks, trimmed and sliced
5 cm/2 inch piece fresh root ginger, peeled and grated
2 green chillies, deseeded and chopped
few curry leaves
1 tsp ground cumin
1 tsp ground coriander
1 tsp turmeric
1 tbsp tomato purée
150 ml/¼ pint water
150 ml/¼ pint coconut milk
225 g/8 oz tomatoes, chopped
450 g/1 lb new potatoes, scrubbed
100 g/3½ oz carrots, peeled and sliced
freshly cooked rice, to serve

Lamb & Date Tagine

1 Place the saffron in a small bowl, cover with warm water and leave to infuse for 10 minutes. Heat the oil in a large, heavy-based pan, add the onion, garlic and lamb and sauté for 8–10 minutes, or until sealed. Add the cinnamon stick and ground cumin and cook, stirring constantly, for a further 2 minutes.

2 Add the carrots and sweet potato, then add the saffron with the soaking liquid and the stock. Bring to the boil, season to taste with salt and pepper, then reduce the heat to a simmer. Cover with a lid and simmer for 45 minutes, stirring occasionally.

3 Add the dates and continue to simmer for a further 15 minutes. Remove the cinnamon stick, adjust the seasoning and serve with freshly prepared couscous.

Ingredients   SERVES 4

few saffron strands
1 tbsp olive oil
1 onion, peeled and cut into wedges
2–3 garlic cloves, peeled and sliced
550 g/1¼ lb lean lamb such as neck
    fillet, diced
1 cinnamon stick, bruised
1 tsp ground cumin
225 g/8 oz carrots, peeled and sliced
350 g/12 oz sweet potato, peeled
    and diced
900 ml/1½ pints lamb or vegetable
    stock
salt and freshly ground black pepper
100 g/3½ oz dates (fresh or dried),
    pitted and halved
freshly prepared couscous, to serve

Tasty Tip
Replace the dates with chopped ready-to-eat dried apricots.

Cornish Pasties

1 Preheat the oven to 180°C/350°F/Gas Mark 4, about 15 minutes before required. To make the pastry, sift the flour into a large bowl and add the fats, chopped into little pieces. Rub the fats and flour together until the mixture resembles coarse breadcrumbs. Season to taste with salt and pepper and mix again.

2 Add about 2 tablespoons of cold water, a little at a time, and mix until the mixture comes together to form a firm but pliable dough. Turn onto a lightly floured surface, knead until smooth, then wrap and chill in the refrigerator.

3 To make the filling, put the braising steak in a large bowl with the onion. Add the potatoes and swede to the bowl together with the Worcestershire sauce and salt and pepper. Mix well.

4 Divide the dough into 8 balls and roll each ball into a circle about 25.5 cm/10 inches across. Divide the filling between the circles of pastry. Wet the edge of the pastry, then fold over the filling. Pinch the edges to seal.

5 Transfer the pasties to a lightly oiled baking sheet. Make a couple of small holes in each pasty and brush with beaten egg. Cook in the preheated oven for 15 minutes, remove and brush again with the egg. Return to the oven for a further 15–20 minutes until golden. Cool slightly, garnish with tomato and parsley and serve.

Ingredients   MAKES 8

For the pastry:

350 g/12 oz self-raising flour
75 g/3 oz butter or margarine
75 g/3 oz lard or white vegetable fat
salt and freshly ground black pepper

For the filling:

550 g/1¼ lb braising steak, very
    finely chopped
1 large onion, peeled and finely
    chopped
1 large potato, peeled and diced
200 g/7 oz swede, peeled and diced
3 tbsp Worcestershire sauce
1 small egg, beaten, to glaze

To garnish:

tomato slices or wedges
sprigs of fresh parsley

Tasty Tip

The shortcrust pastry for these pasties is made with self-raising flour, which gives it a softer, lighter texture.

Seared Calves' Liver with Onions & Mustard Mash

1 Preheat the oven to 150°C/300°F/Gas Mark 2. Heat half the oil and 25 g/1 oz of the butter in a flameproof casserole. When foaming, add the onions. Cover and cook over a low heat for 20 minutes until softened and beginning to collapse. Add the sugar and season with salt and pepper. Stir in the thyme. Cover the casserole and transfer to the preheated oven. Cook for a further 30–45 minutes until softened completely, but not browned. Remove from the oven and stir in the balsamic vinegar.

2 Meanwhile, boil the potatoes in boiling salted water for 15–18 minutes until tender. Drain well, then return to the pan. Place over a low heat to dry completely, remove from the heat and stir in 50 g/2 oz of the butter, the milk, mustard and salt and pepper to taste. Mash thoroughly until creamy and keep warm.

3 Heat a large frying pan and add the remaining butter and oil. When it is foaming, add the mustard and sage leaves and stir for a few seconds, then add the liver. Cook over a high heat for 1–2 minutes on each side. It should remain slightly pink: do not overcook. Remove the liver from the pan. Add the lemon juice to the pan and swirl around to deglaze.

4 To serve, place a large spoonful of the mashed potato on each plate. Top with some of the melting onions, the liver and finally the pan juices.

Ingredients SERVES 2

2 tbsp olive oil
100 g/3½ oz butter
3 large onions, peeled and finely sliced
pinch of sugar
salt and freshly ground black pepper
1 tbsp sprigs of fresh thyme
1 tbsp balsamic vinegar
700 g/1½ lb potatoes, peeled and
    cut into chunks
6–8 tbsp milk
1 tbsp wholegrain mustard
3–4 fresh sage leaves
550 g/1¼ lb thinly sliced calves' liver
1 tsp lemon juice

Helpful Hint

Calves' liver is mild and tender and needs only brief cooking over a high heat to sear the outside, but keep it moist and juicy within. Lambs' liver may be used for this recipe instead, but tone down the slightly stronger flavour by soaking in milk for up to 1 hour before cooking.

Marinated Lamb Chops with Garlic Fried Potatoes

1 Trim the chops of any excess fat, wipe with a clean damp cloth and reserve. To make the marinade, using a pestle and mortar, pound the thyme leaves and rosemary with the salt until pulpy. Add the garlic and continue pounding until crushed. Stir in the lemon rind and juice and the olive oil.

2 Pour the marinade over the lamb chops, turning them until they are well coated. Cover lightly and leave to marinate in the refrigerator for about 1 hour.

3 Meanwhile, heat the oil in a large nonstick frying pan. Add the potatoes and garlic and cook over a low heat for about 20 minutes, stirring occasionally. Increase the heat and cook for a further 10–15 minutes until golden. Drain on absorbent kitchen paper and add salt to taste. Keep warm.

4 Heat a griddle pan until almost smoking. Add the lamb chops and cook for 3–4 minutes on each side until golden, but still pink in the middle. Serve with the potatoes and either a mixed salad or freshly cooked vegetables.

Ingredients   SERVES 4

4 thick lamb chump chops
3 tbsp olive oil
550 g/1$^{1}/_{4}$ lb potatoes, peeled and
    cut into 1 cm/$^{1}/_{2}$ inch dice
6 unpeeled garlic cloves
mixed salad or freshly cooked
    vegetables, to serve

For the marinade:

1 small bunch fresh thyme,
    leaves removed
1 tbsp freshly chopped rosemary
1 tsp salt
2 garlic cloves, peeled and crushed
rind and juice of 1 lemon
2 tbsp olive oil

Tasty Tip

Marinating the chops not only adds flavour, but tenderises as well, due to the acids in the lemon juice. If time allows, marinate the chops for slightly longer. Try other citrus juices for a change, such as orange or lime.

Beef Bourguignon

1. Preheat the oven 160°C/325°F/Gas Mark 3. Cut the steak and pork into small pieces and reserve. Heat 1 tablespoon of the oil in an ovenproof casserole (or frying pan, if preferred), add the meat and cook in batches for 5–8 minutes, or until sealed. Remove with a slotted spoon and reserve.

2. Add the remaining oil to the casserole/pan, then add the shallots, carrots and garlic and cook for 10 minutes. Return the meat to the casserole/pan and sprinkle in the flour. Cook for 2 minutes, stirring occasionally, before pouring in the brandy, if using. Heat for 1 minute, then take off the heat and ignite.

3. When the flames have subsided, pour in the wine and stock. Return to the heat and bring to the boil, stirring constantly.

4. If a frying pan has been used, transfer everything to a casserole, add the bay leaf and season to taste with salt and pepper. Cover with a lid and cook in the oven for 1 hour.

5. Cut the potatoes in half. Remove the casserole from the oven and add the potatoes. Cook for a further 1 hour, or until the meat and potatoes are tender. Serve sprinkled with chopped parsley.

Ingredients   SERVES 4

700 g/1½ lb braising steak, trimmed
225 g/8 oz piece pork belly or
    lardons
2 tbsp olive oil
12 shallots, peeled
2 garlic cloves, peeled and sliced
225 g/8 oz carrots, peeled and sliced
2 tbsp plain flour
3 tbsp brandy (optional)
150 ml/¼ pint red wine, such as a
    Burgundy
450 ml/¾ pint beef stock
1 bay leaf
salt and freshly ground black pepper
450 g/1 lb new potatoes, scrubbed
1 tbsp freshly chopped parsley,
    to garnish

Tasty Tip
If time allows, increase the wine to 300 ml/½ pint and marinate the beef in the refrigerator overnight.

Steak & Kidney Stew

1 Heat the oil in a large, heavy-based saucepan, add the onion, garlic and celery and sauté for 5 minutes, or until browned. Remove from the pan with a slotted spoon and reserve.

2 Add the steak and kidneys to the pan and cook for 3–5 minutes, or until sealed, then return the onion mixture to the pan. Sprinkle in the flour and cook, stirring, for 2 minutes. Take off the heat, stir in the tomato purée, then the stock, and season to taste with salt and pepper. Add the bay leaf.

3 Return to the heat and bring to the boil, stirring occasionally. Add the carrots, then reduce the heat to a simmer and cover with a lid. Cook for 1¼ hours, stirring occasionally. Reduce the heat if the liquid is evaporating quickly. Add the potatoes and cook for a further 30 minutes.

4 Place the flour, suet and herbs in a bowl and add a little seasoning. Add the water and mix to a stiff mixture. Using a little extra flour, shape into 8 small balls. Place the dumplings on top of the stew, cover with the lid and continue to cook for 15 minutes, or until the meat is tender and the dumplings are well risen and fluffy. Stir in the spinach and leave to stand for 2 minutes, or until the spinach is wilted, before serving.

Ingredients   SERVES 4

1 tbsp olive oil
1 onion, peeled and chopped
2–3 garlic cloves, peeled and crushed
2 celery sticks, trimmed and sliced
550 g/1¼ lb braising steak, trimmed and diced
100 g/3½ oz lambs' or pigs' kidneys, cored and chopped
2 tbsp plain flour
1 tbsp tomato purée
900 ml/1½ pints beef stock
salt and freshly ground black pepper
1 fresh bay leaf
300 g/10 oz carrots, peeled and sliced
350 g/12 oz baby new potatoes, scrubbed
350 g/12 oz fresh spinach leaves, chopped

For the dumplings:

100 g/3½ oz self-raising flour
50 g/2 oz shredded suet
1 tbsp freshly chopped mixed herbs
2–3 tbsp water

Massaman Beef Curry

1 Trim the beef, cut into thin strips and reserve. Heat 2 tablespoons of the oil in a heavy-based saucepan, add the ginger and chillies and fry for 3 minutes. Add the onions and garlic and continue to fry for 5 minutes, or until the onions have softened.

2 Remove the mixture with a slotted spoon and add the beef to the pan. Cook, stirring, for 5 minutes, or until sealed.

3 Add the curry paste and continue to fry for 3 minutes, then return the ginger, chillies, onions and garlic to the pan and stir well.

4 Pour the coconut milk and stock into the pan and bring to the boil. Reduce the heat, cover and simmer for 30 minutes, stirring occasionally.

5 Add the potatoes to the pan, with more stock if necessary, then continue to simmer for 20–25 minutes, or until the meat and potatoes are cooked. Meanwhile, heat the remaining oil in a small saucepan, add the green pepper strips and fry for 2 minutes. Add the chopped peanuts and fry for 1 minute, stirring constantly. Sprinkle over the cooked curry and serve.

Ingredients SERVES 4–6

450 g/1 lb beef steak, such as sirloin
  or rump
3 tbsp vegetable oil
5 cm/2 inch piece fresh root ginger,
  peeled and grated
3 green bird's eye chillies, deseeded
  and chopped
2 red onions, peeled and chopped
3 garlic cloves, peeled and crushed
2 tbsp Massaman Thai curry paste
400 ml/14 fl oz coconut milk
150–200 ml/5–7 fl oz beef stock
350 g/12 oz new potatoes, scrubbed
  and cut into small chunks
1 green pepper, deseeded and cut
  into strips
50 g/2 oz roasted peanuts, chopped

Helpful Hint

If a hotter curry is preferred, increase the number of chillies and add 1 tablespoon of chilli powder when frying the onions and garlic.

Chilli Con Carne with Crispy-skinned Potatoes

1 Preheat the oven to 150°C/300°F/Gas Mark 2. Heat the oil in a large flameproof casserole and add the onion. Cook gently for 10 minutes until soft and lightly browned. Add the garlic and chilli and cook briefly. Increase the heat. Add the chuck steak or lean mince and cook for a further 10 minutes, stirring occasionally, until browned.

2 Add the chilli powder and stir well. Cook for about 2 minutes, then add the chopped tomatoes and tomato purée. Bring slowly to the boil. Cover and cook in the preheated oven for 1¹/₂ hours. Remove from the oven and stir in the kidney beans. Return to the oven for a further 15 minutes.

3 Meanwhile, brush a little vegetable oil all over the potatoes and rub on some coarse salt. Put the potatoes in the oven alongside the chilli.

4 Remove the chilli and potatoes from the oven. Cut a cross in each potato, then squeeze to open slightly and season to taste with salt and pepper. Serve with the chilli, guacamole and soured cream.

Ingredients SERVES 4

2 tbsp vegetable oil, plus extra
for brushing
1 large onion, peeled and
finely chopped
1 garlic clove, peeled and
finely chopped
1 red chilli, deseeded and
finely chopped
450 g/1 lb chuck steak, finely
chopped, or lean beef mince
1 tbsp chilli powder
400 g can chopped tomatoes
2 tbsp tomato purée
400 g can red kidney beans, drained
and rinsed
4 large baking potatoes
coarse salt and freshly ground
black pepper

To serve:
ready-made guacamole
soured cream

Grilled Steaks with Saffron Potatoes & Roast Tomatoes

1 Cook the potatoes in boiling salted water for 8 minutes and drain well. Return the potatoes to the saucepan along with the saffron, stock, onion and 25 g/1 oz of the butter. Season to taste with salt and pepper and simmer, uncovered, for 10 minutes until the potatoes are tender.

2 Meanwhile, preheat the grill to medium. Mix together the vinegar, olive oil, sugar and seasoning. Arrange the tomatoes cut-side up in a foil-lined grill pan and drizzle over the dressing. Grill for 12–15 minutes, basting occasionally, until tender.

3 Melt the remaining butter in a frying pan. Add the steaks and cook for 4–8 minutes to taste and depending on thickness.

4 Arrange the potatoes and tomatoes in the centres of 4 serving plates. Top with the steaks along with any pan juices. Sprinkle over the parsley and serve immediately.

Ingredients   SERVES 4

700 g/1½ lb new potatoes, halved
few strands of saffron
300 ml/½ pint vegetable or beef stock
1 small onion, peeled and finely chopped
75 g/3 oz butter
salt and freshly ground black pepper
2 tsp balsamic vinegar
2 tbsp olive oil
1 tsp caster sugar
8 plum tomatoes, halved
4 boneless sirloin steaks, each weighing
    225 g/8 oz
2 tbsp freshly chopped parsley

Helpful Hint

You can tell how well a steak is cooked by lightly pressing with your fingertips – the less the resistance, the rarer the meat. As a rough guide, a 2 cm/¾ inch thick steak will take about 2 minutes on each side for rare, 3–4 minutes on each side for medium and 6–7 minutes on each side for well-done.

Pork Sausages with Onion Gravy & Best-ever Mash

1 Melt the butter with the oil and add the onions. Cover and cook gently for about 20 minutes until the onions have collapsed. Add the sugar and stir well. Uncover and continue to cook, stirring often, until the onions are very soft and golden. Add the thyme, stir well, then add the flour, stirring. Gradually add the Madeira and the stock. Bring to the boil and simmer gently for 10 minutes.

2 Meanwhile, put the sausages in a large frying pan and cook over a medium heat for about 15–20 minutes, turning often, until golden brown and slightly sticky all over.

3 For the mash, boil the potatoes in plenty of lightly salted water for 15–18 minutes until tender. Drain well and return to the saucepan. Put the saucepan over a low heat to allow the potatoes to dry thoroughly. Remove from the heat and add the butter, crème fraîche and salt and pepper. Mash thoroughly. Serve the potato mash topped with the sausages and onion gravy.

Ingredients   SERVES 4

50 g/2 oz butter
1 tbsp olive oil
2 large onions, peeled and thinly sliced
pinch of sugar
1 tbsp freshly chopped thyme
1 tbsp plain flour
100 ml/3¹/₂ fl oz Madeira
200 ml/7 fl oz vegetable stock
8–12 good-quality butchers' pork
    sausages, depending on size

For the mash:

900 g/2 lb floury potatoes, peeled
75 g/3 oz butter
4 tbsp crème fraîche or soured cream
salt and freshly ground black pepper

Helpful Hint

Sausages should always be cooked slowly over a gentle heat to ensure that they are cooked through.

Sausage & Apple Pot

1   Preheat the oven to 180˚C/350˚F/Gas Mark 4. Heat the oil in an ovenproof casserole (or frying pan, if preferred), add the onion, garlic and celery and sauté for 5 minutes. Push the vegetables to one side, then add the sausages and cook, turning the sausages over, until browned.

2   If a frying pan has been used, transfer everything to a casserole. Arrange the onions over and around the sausages together with the carrots, apple and courgettes. Season to taste with salt and pepper and pour over the stock. Sprinkle with the mixed herbs, cover with a lid and cook in the oven for 30 minutes.

3   Meanwhile, soak the grated potatoes in a bowl of cold water for 10 minutes. Drain thoroughly, then place the potatoes on a clean tea towel and squeeze to remove any excess moisture.

4   Remove the casserole from the oven and place the grated potatoes on top. Sprinkle with the grated cheese, then return to the oven and cook for 30 minutes, or until the vegetables are tender and the topping is crisp.

Ingredients   SERVES 4

1 tbsp olive oil

1 onion, peeled and sliced

2–3 garlic cloves, peeled and sliced

2 celery sticks, trimmed and sliced

8 apple and pork flavoured
  thick sausages

300 g/10 oz carrots, peeled and sliced

1 large cooking apple, peeled and
  sliced

300 g/10 oz courgettes, trimmed
  and sliced

salt and freshly ground black pepper

600 ml/1 pint vegetable stock

2 tsp dried mixed herbs

450 g/1 lb potatoes, peeled and grated

50 g/2 oz Gruyère cheese, grated

Tasty Tip

Other flavoured sausages can be used according to personal preference, such as herb, chilli or Cumberland. Vegetarian sausages can also be used.

Roast Cured Pork Loin with Baked Sliced Potatoes

1 Preheat the oven to 190°C/375°F/Gas Mark 5. Mix together the mustard, honey and black pepper. Spread evenly over the pork loin. Place in the centre of a large square of foil and wrap loosely. Cook in the preheated oven for 15 minutes per 450 g/1 lb, plus an extra 15 minutes (45 minutes), unwrapping the joint for the last 30 minutes of cooking time.

2 Meanwhile, layer one-third of the potatoes, one-third of the butter, half the onions and half the flour in a large gratin dish. Add half the remaining potatoes and butter and the remaining onions and flour. Finally, cover with the remaining potatoes. Season well with salt and pepper between layers. Pour in the milk and dot with the remaining butter. Cover the dish loosely with foil and put in the oven below the pork. Cook for 1¹/₂ hours.

3 Remove the foil from the potatoes and cook for a further 20 minutes until tender and golden. Remove the pork loin from the oven and leave to rest for 10 minutes before carving thinly. Serve with the potatoes and a fresh green salad.

Ingredients   SERVES 4

2 tbsp wholegrain mustard
2 tbsp clear honey
1 tsp coarsely crushed black pepper
900 g/2 lb piece smoked cured
  pork loin
900 g/2 lb potatoes, peeled and
  thinly sliced
75 g/3 oz butter, diced
1 large onion, peeled and
  finely chopped
25 g/1 oz plain flour
salt and freshly ground black pepper
600 ml/1 pint milk
fresh green salad, to serve

Helpful Hint

Smoked cured pork loin can be found in specialist butchers and is delicately flavoured. If you are unable to find it, an ordinary piece of pork loin can be used here. It usually has a good layer of crackling, so remove it for this recipe, sprinkle with a little salt and cook separately under the grill.

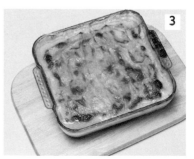

Crispy Baked Potatoes with Serrano Ham

1 Preheat the oven to 200°C/400°F/Gas Mark 6. Scrub the potatoes dry. Prick with a fork and place on a baking sheet. Cook for 1–1½ hours, or until tender when squeezed. (Use oven gloves or a kitchen towel to pick up the potatoes as they will be very hot.)

2 Cut the potatoes in half horizontally and scoop out all the flesh into a bowl.

3 Spoon the crème fraîche into the bowl and mix thoroughly with the potatoes. Season to taste with a little salt and pepper.

4 Cut the ham into strips and carefully stir into the potato mixture with the broad beans, carrots and peas.

5 Pile the mixture back into the 8 potato shells and sprinkle a little grated cheese on the top.

6 Place under a hot grill and cook until golden and heated through. Serve immediately with a fresh green salad.

Ingredients   SERVES 4

4 large baking potatoes
4 tsp half-fat crème fraîche
salt and freshly ground black pepper
50 g/2 oz lean serrano ham or
     prosciutto, with fat removed
50 g/2 oz cooked baby broad beans
50 g/2 oz cooked carrots, diced
50 g/2 oz cooked peas
50 g/2 oz low-fat hard cheese, such
     as Edam or Cheddar, grated
fresh green salad, to serve

Food Fact

Produced in Spain, serrano ham has a succulent sweet taste and is traditionally carved along the grain. The nearest substitute is prosciutto. Serrano ham has a chewy texture and is often served in thin slices on bread.

Lemon Chicken with Potatoes, Rosemary & Olives

1 Preheat the oven to 200°C/400°F/Gas Mark 6, 15 minutes before cooking. Trim the chicken thighs and place in a shallow baking dish large enough to hold them in a single layer. Remove the rind from the lemon with a zester or, if using a peeler, cut into thin julienne strips. Reserve half and add the remainder to the chicken. Squeeze the lemon juice over the chicken, toss to coat well and leave to stand for 10 minutes.

2 Add the remaining lemon zest or julienne strips, olive oil, garlic, onions and half the rosemary sprigs. Toss gently and leave for about 20 minutes.

3 Cover the potatoes with lightly salted water and bring to the boil. Cook for 2 minutes, then drain well and add to the chicken. Season to taste with salt and pepper.

4 Roast the chicken in the preheated oven for 50 minutes or until it is cooked, turning frequently and basting. Just before the end of the cooking time, discard the rosemary and add fresh sprigs of rosemary. Add the olives and stir. Serve immediately with steamed carrots and courgettes.

Ingredients   SERVES 6

12 skinless, boneless chicken thighs
1 large lemon
125 ml/4 fl oz extra virgin olive oil
6 garlic cloves, peeled and sliced
2 onions, peeled and thinly sliced
bunch of fresh rosemary
1.1 kg/2½ lb potatoes, peeled and
    cut into 4 cm/1½ inch pieces
salt and freshly ground black pepper
18–24 black olives, pitted

To serve:
steamed carrots
courgettes

Helpful Hint

It is worth seeking out unwaxed lemons for this recipe, or for any recipe in which the lemon zest is to be eaten. If unwaxed fruit are unavailable, pour hot water over them and scrub well before removing the zest.

Chicken & New Potatoes on Rosemary Skewers

1 Preheat the grill and line the grill rack with foil just before cooking. Strip the leaves from the rosemary stems, leaving about 5 cm/2 inches of soft leaves at the top. Chop the leaves coarsely and reserve. Using a sharp knife, cut the thicker woody ends of the stems to a point which can pierce the chicken pieces and potatoes. Blend the chopped rosemary, oil, garlic, thyme and lemon rind and juice in a shallow dish. Season to taste with salt and pepper. Cut the chicken into 4 cm/1½ inch cubes, add to the flavoured oil and stir well. Cover and refrigerate for at least 30 minutes, turning occasionally. Cook the potatoes in lightly salted boiling water for 10–12 minutes until just tender. Add the onions to the potatoes 2 minutes before the end of the cooking time. Drain, rinse under cold running water and leave to cool. Cut the pepper into 2.5 cm/1 inch squares.

2 Beginning with a piece of chicken and starting with the pointed end of the skewer, alternately thread equal amounts of chicken, potato, pepper and onion onto each rosemary skewer. Cover the leafy ends of the skewers with foil to stop them from burning. Do not thread the chicken and vegetables too closely together on the skewer or the chicken may not cook completely. Cook the kebabs for 15 minutes, or until tender and golden, turning and brushing with either extra oil or the marinade. Remove the foil, garnish with lemon wedges and serve on rice.

Ingredients SERVES 4

8 thick fresh rosemary stems, at least
   23 cm/9 inches long
3–4 tbsp extra virgin olive oil
2 garlic cloves, peeled and crushed
1 tsp freshly chopped thyme
grated rind and juice of 1 lemon
salt and freshly ground black pepper
4 skinless chicken breast fillets
16 small new potatoes, peeled or
   scrubbed
8 very small onions or shallots, peeled
1 large yellow or red pepper, deseeded
lemon wedges, to garnish
parsley-flavoured cooked rice, to serve

Tasty Tip

Threading the chicken and vegetables onto fresh rosemary stems will subtly flavour them and give a wonderful aroma during cooking. Soak the skewers in cold water for about 15 minutes before adding the food; this will prevent them from burning while they are under the grill or on the barbecue.

Chicken Pie with Sweet Potato Topping

1 Preheat the oven to 190°C/375°F/Gas Mark 5, 10 minutes
before required. Cook the potatoes in lightly salted boiling
water until tender. Drain well, then return to the saucepan and
mash until smooth and creamy, gradually adding the milk, then
the butter, sugar and orange rind. Season to taste with salt and
pepper and reserve.

2 Place the chicken in a saucepan with the onion, mushrooms,
leeks, wine and stock cube and season to taste. Simmer,
covered, until the chicken and vegetables are tender. Using a
slotted spoon, transfer the chicken and vegetables to a 1.1
litre/2 pint pie dish. Add the parsley and crème fraîche or
cream to the liquid in the pan and bring to the boil. Simmer
until thickened and smooth, stirring constantly. Pour over the
chicken in the pie dish, mix and cool.

3 Spread the mashed potato over the chicken filling and swirl the
surface into decorative peaks. Bake in the preheated oven for
35 minutes, or until the top is golden and the chicken filling is
heated through. Serve immediately with fresh green vegetables.

Ingredients SERVES 4

700 g/1½ lb sweet potatoes, peeled
and cut into chunks
salt and freshly ground black pepper
250 g/9 oz potatoes, peeled and cut
into chunks
150 ml/¼ pint milk
25 g/1 oz butter
2 tsp brown sugar
grated rind of 1 orange
4 skinless chicken breast fillets, diced
1 medium onion, peeled and
coarsely chopped
125 g/4 oz baby mushrooms, stems
trimmed
2 leeks, trimmed and thickly sliced
150 ml/¼ pint dry white wine
1 chicken stock cube
1 tbsp freshly chopped parsley
50 ml/2 fl oz crème fraîche or thick
double cream
green vegetables, to serve

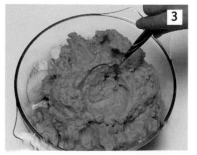

Warm Chicken & Potato Salad with Peas & Mint

1   Cook the potatoes in lightly salted boiling water for 15 minutes, or until just tender when pierced with the tip of a sharp knife; do not overcook. Rinse under cold running water to cool slightly, then drain and turn into a large bowl. Sprinkle with the cider vinegar and toss gently.

2   Run the peas under hot water to ensure that they are thawed, pat dry with absorbent kitchen paper and add to the potatoes.

3   Cut the avocado in half lengthways and remove the stone. Peel and cut the avocado into cubes and add to the potatoes and peas. Add the chicken and stir together lightly.

4   To make the dressing, place all the ingredients in a screw-top jar, with a little salt and pepper and shake well to mix; add a little more oil if the flavour is too sharp. Pour over the salad and toss gently to coat. Sprinkle in half the mint and stir lightly.

5   Separate the lettuce leaves and spread onto a large shallow serving plate. Spoon the salad on top and sprinkle with the remaining mint. Garnish with mint sprigs and serve.

Ingredients   SERVES 4–6

450 g/1 lb new potatoes, peeled
  or scrubbed and cut into
  bite-size pieces
salt and freshly ground black pepper
2 tbsp cider vinegar
175 g/6 oz frozen garden
  peas, thawed
1 small ripe avocado
4 cooked chicken breasts, about 450
  g/1 lb in weight, skinned and diced
2 tbsp freshly chopped mint
2 heads Little Gem lettuce
fresh mint sprigs, to garnish

For the dressing:

2 tbsp raspberry or sherry vinegar
2 tsp Dijon mustard
1 tsp clear honey
50 ml/2 fl oz sunflower oil
50 ml/2 fl oz extra virgin olive oil

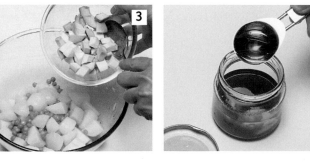

Slow Roast Chicken with Potatoes & Oregano

1 Preheat the oven to 200°C/400°F/Gas Mark 6. Rinse the chicken and dry well, inside and out, with absorbent kitchen paper. Rub the chicken all over with the lemon halves, then squeeze the juice over it and into the cavity. Put the lemon into the cavity with the quartered onion. Rub the softened butter all over the chicken and season, then put it in a large roasting tin, breast-side down.

2 Toss the potatoes in the oil, season with salt and pepper to taste and add the dried oregano and fresh thyme. Arrange the potatoes with the oil around the chicken and carefully pour 150 ml/¼ pint water into one end of the pan (not over the oil). Roast in the preheated oven for 25 minutes. Reduce the oven temperature to 190°C/375°F/Gas Mark 5 and turn the chicken breast-side up. Turn the potatoes, sprinkle over half the fresh herbs and baste the chicken and potatoes with the juices. Continue roasting for 1 hour, or until the chicken is cooked, basting occasionally. If the liquid evaporates completely, add a little more water.

3 The chicken is done when the juices run clear when the thigh is pierced with a skewer. Transfer the chicken to a carving board and rest for 5 minutes, covered with foil. Return the potatoes to the oven while the chicken is resting. Carve the chicken into serving pieces and arrange on a large heatproof serving dish. Arrange the potatoes around the chicken and drizzle over any remaining juices. Sprinkle with the remaining herbs and serve.

Ingredients SERVES 6

1.4–1.8 kg/3–4 lb oven-ready chicken, preferably free range
1 lemon, halved
1 onion, peeled and quartered
50 g/2 oz butter, softened
salt and freshly ground black pepper
1 kg/2¼ lb potatoes, peeled and quartered
3–4 tbsp extra virgin olive oil
1 tbsp dried oregano, crumbled
1 tsp fresh thyme leaves
2 tbsp freshly chopped thyme
fresh sage leaves, to garnish

Tasty Tip

Roasting the chicken breast-side down for the first 25 minutes of cooking allows the fat and juices to run into the breast, keeping it moist.
It is important to baste the chicken now and then, once it is turned, so that the breast does not dry out.

Herbed Hasselback Potatoes with Roast Chicken

1 Preheat the oven to 200°C/400°F/Gas Mark 6, about 15 minutes before cooking. Place a chopstick on either side of a potato and, with a sharp knife, cut down through the potato until you reach the chopsticks; take care not to cut right through the potato. Repeat these cuts every 5 mm/$^1/_4$ inch along the length of the potato. Carefully ease 2–4 of the slices apart and slip in a few rosemary sprigs. Repeat with the remaining potatoes. Brush with the oil and season well with salt and pepper.

2 Place the seasoned potatoes in a large roasting tin. Add the parsnips, carrots and leeks to the potatoes in the tin and cover with a wire rack or trivet.

3 Beat the butter and lemon rind together and season to taste. Smear the chicken with the lemon butter and place on the rack over the vegetables.

4 Roast in the preheated oven for 1 hour 40 minutes, basting the chicken and vegetables occasionally, until cooked thoroughly. The juices should run clear when the thigh is pierced with a skewer. Place the cooked chicken on a warmed serving platter, arrange the roast vegetables around it and serve immediately.

Ingredients   SERVES 4

8 medium, evenly-sized potatoes, peeled
3 large sprigs of fresh rosemary
1 tbsp olive oil (not extra virgin)
salt and freshly ground black pepper
350 g/12 oz baby parsnips, peeled
350 g/12 oz baby carrots, peeled
350 g/12 oz baby leeks, trimmed
75 g/3 oz butter
finely grated rind of 1 lemon, preferably unwaxed
1.6 kg/3$^1/_2$ lb chicken

Food Fact

Hasselback potatoes were named after the Stockholm restaurant of the same name. Using chopsticks is a great way of ensuring that you slice just far enough through the potatoes so that they fan out during cooking. The potatoes can be given an attractive golden finish by mixing $^1/_4$ tsp ground turmeric or paprika with the oil.

Spiced Indian Roast Potatoes with Chicken

1 Preheat the oven to 190°C/375°F/Gas Mark 5, about 10 minutes before cooking. Parboil the potatoes for 5 minutes in lightly salted boiling water, then drain thoroughly and reserve. Heat the oil in a large frying pan, add the chicken drumsticks and cook until sealed on all sides. Remove and reserve.

2 Add the onion and shallots to the pan and fry for 4–5 minutes, or until softened. Stir in the garlic, chilli and ginger and cook for 1 minute, stirring constantly. Stir in the ground cumin, coriander, cayenne pepper and crushed cardamom pods and continue to cook, stirring, for a further minute.

3 Add the potatoes to the pan, then add the chicken. Season to taste with salt and pepper. Stir gently until the potatoes and chicken pieces are coated in the onion and spice mixture.

4 Spoon into a large roasting tin and roast in the preheated oven for 35 minutes, or until the chicken and potatoes are cooked thoroughly. Garnish with fresh coriander and serve immediately.

Ingredients   SERVES 4

700 g/1½ lb waxy potatoes, peeled and
    cut into large chunks
salt and freshly ground black pepper
4 tbsp sunflower oil
8 chicken drumsticks
1 large Spanish onion, peeled and
    roughly chopped
3 shallots, peeled and roughly chopped
2 large garlic cloves, peeled and crushed
1 red chilli
2 tsp fresh root ginger, peeled and
    finely grated
2 tsp ground cumin
2 tsp ground coriander
pinch of cayenne pepper
4 cardamom pods, crushed
sprigs of fresh coriander, to garnish

Handy Hint

Spanish onions are the largest white onions and they have a much milder flavour than smaller English ones.

Creole Chicken Curry

1. Preheat the oven to 190°C/375°F/Gas Mark 5. Place half the garlic in a food processor with the salt, citrus rind and fresh herbs and blend to form a paste.

2. Skin the chicken portions, if preferred, and make small incisions into the flesh. Insert the remaining garlic into the incisions and spread with the prepared herb paste. Place on a plate, cover lightly and leave to marinate in the refrigerator for at least 30 minutes.

3. When ready to cook, heat the oil in a frying pan, add the chicken and brown on all sides. Remove and place in an ovenproof casserole. Add the curry paste with the tamarind paste, Worcestershire sauce and sugar and cook, stirring, for 2 minutes. Add the sweet potato chunks with the juice and stock and bring to the boil. Boil gently, stirring, for 2 minutes, add the curry leaves, then pour over the chicken.

4. Cover with a lid and cook in the preheated oven for 30 minutes. Add the sugar snaps and cook for a further 5–8 minutes, or until the chicken is thoroughly cooked. Serve sprinkled with chopped coriander.

Ingredients   SERVES 4–6

8 garlic cloves, peeled and cut in half
$1/2$ tsp salt
1 tbsp grated lime or lemon rind
1 tbsp fresh thyme leaves
1 tbsp fresh oregano leaves
2 tsp freshly chopped coriander
4 chicken thighs
2 tbsp vegetable oil
1 tbsp curry paste
1 tbsp tamarind paste
1 tbsp Worcestershire sauce
2 tsp demerara sugar
350 g/12 oz sweet potatoes, peeled and cut into small chunks
250 ml/8 fl oz orange or mango juice
150 ml/$1/4$ pint chicken stock
few curry leaves
100 g/$31/2$ oz sugar snap peas
2 tbsp freshly chopped coriander, to garnish

Tasty Tip

If you can find dried tamarind, soak 75 g/3 oz in 350 ml/12 fl oz water and use in place of the orange juice and stock.

Chicken Marengo Casserole

1 Preheat the oven to 180°C/350°F/Gas Mark 4. Lightly rinse the chicken and pat dry on absorbent kitchen paper.

2 Heat the oil and butter in an ovenproof casserole (or frying pan, if preferred), add the chicken portions and cook until browned all over. Remove with a slotted spoon and reserve.

3 Add the onion and garlic and cook gently for 5 minutes, stirring occasionally. Sprinkle in the flour and cook for 2 minutes before stirring in the stock and bringing to the boil.

4 If a frying pan has been used, transfer everything to a casserole and return the chicken to the casserole with the peeled tomatoes. Season to taste with salt and pepper and add the bay leaf. Cover with a lid and cook in the oven for 30 minutes. Remove the casserole from the oven and add the potatoes and sweetcorn. Return to the oven and cook for 30 minutes. Add the spinach and stir gently through the casserole. Return to the oven and cook for a further 10 minutes, or until the spinach has wilted. Serve.

Ingredients   SERVES 4

4 chicken portions, skinned
1 tbsp olive oil
15 g/¹/₂ oz unsalted butter
1 onion, peeled and cut into wedges
2–3 garlic cloves, peeled and sliced
2 tbsp plain flour
900 ml/1¹/₂ pints chicken stock
300 g/10 oz tomatoes, peeled
salt and freshly ground black pepper
1 fresh bay leaf
350 g/12 oz new potatoes, scrubbed
    and cut in half
75 g/3 oz sweetcorn kernels
350 g/12 oz fresh spinach

Helpful Hint

This can also be made using half chicken stock and half wine. Use a dry white such as Chardonnay or Pinot Grigio.

Chicken Chasseur

1 Preheat the oven to 180°C/350°F/Gas Mark 4. Skin the chicken, if preferred, and rinse lightly. Pat dry on absorbent kitchen paper. Heat the oil and butter in an ovenproof casserole (or frying pan, if preferred), add the chicken portions and cook, in batches, until browned all over. Remove with a slotted spoon and reserve.

2 Add the onions, garlic and celery to the casserole and cook for 5 minutes, or until golden. Cut the mushrooms in half if large, then add to the casserole and cook for 2 minutes.

3 Sprinkle in the flour and cook for 2 minutes, then gradually stir in the wine. Blend the tomato purée with a little of the stock in a small bowl, then stir into the casserole together with the remaining stock. Bring to the boil, stirring constantly.

4 If a frying pan has been used, transfer everything to a casserole. Return the chicken to the casserole, season to taste and add a few tarragon sprigs.

5 Stir in the sweet potato, cover with a lid and cook in the oven for 30 minutes. Remove the casserole from the oven and add the broad beans. Return to the oven and cook for a further 15–20 minutes, or until the chicken and vegetables are cooked. Serve sprinkled with chopped tarragon.

Ingredients   SERVES 4

1 whole chicken, about 1.5 kg/3 lb in weight, jointed into 4 or 8 portions
1 tbsp olive oil
15 g/½ oz unsalted butter
12 baby onions, peeled
2–4 garlic cloves, peeled and sliced
2 celery sticks, trimmed and sliced
175 g/6 oz closed cup mushrooms, wiped
2 tbsp plain flour
300 ml/½ pint dry white wine
2 tbsp tomato purée
450 ml/¾ pint chicken stock
salt and freshly ground black pepper
few sprigs of fresh tarragon
350 g/12 oz sweet potatoes, peeled and cut into chunks
300 g/10 oz shelled fresh or frozen broad beans
1 tbsp freshly chopped tarragon, to garnish

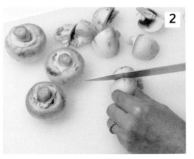

Potato-stuffed Roast Poussin

1 Preheat the oven to 220°C/425°F/Gas Mark 7. Place a roasting tin in the oven to heat. Rinse the poussin cavities and pat dry with absorbent kitchen paper. Season the cavities with salt and pepper and a squeeze of lemon. Push a lemon quarter into each cavity. Put the potatoes in a saucepan of lightly salted water and bring to the boil. Reduce the heat to low and simmer until just tender; do not overcook. Drain and cool slightly. Sprinkle the chopped herbs over the potatoes and drizzle with 2–3 tablespoons of the oil.

2 Spoon half the seasoned potatoes into the poussin cavities; do not pack too tightly. Rub each poussin with a little more oil and season with pepper. Carefully spoon 1 tablespoon of oil into the hot roasting tin and arrange the poussins in the tin. Spoon the remaining potatoes around the edge. Sprinkle over the garlic. Roast the poussins in the preheated oven for 30 minutes, or until the skin is golden and beginning to crisp. Carefully lay the bacon slices over the breast of each poussin and continue to roast for 15–20 minutes until crisp and the poussins are cooked through. Transfer the poussins and potatoes to a serving platter and cover loosely with foil. Skim off the fat from the juices. Place the tin over a medium heat and add the wine and spring onions. Cook briefly, scraping the bits from the bottom of the tin. Whisk in the cream or crème fraîche and bubble for 1 minute, or until thickened. Garnish the poussins with lemon wedges and serve with the creamy gravy.

Ingredients   SERVES 4

4 oven-ready poussins
salt and freshly ground black pepper
1 lemon, cut into quarters
450 g/1 lb floury potatoes, peeled and
  cut into 4 cm/1$\frac{1}{2}$ inch pieces
1 tbsp freshly chopped thyme
  or rosemary
3–4 tbsp olive oil
4 garlic cloves, unpeeled and lightly
  smashed
8 slices streaky bacon or Parma ham
125 ml/4 fl oz white wine
2 spring onions, trimmed and
  thinly sliced
2 tbsp double cream or crème fraîche
lemon wedges, to garnish

Turkey Hash with Potato & Beetroot

1 In a large, heavy-based frying pan, heat the oil and half the butter over a medium heat until sizzling. Add the bacon and cook for 4 minutes, or until crisp and golden, stirring occasionally. Using a slotted spoon, transfer to a large bowl. Add the onion to the pan and cook for 3–4 minutes, or until soft and golden, stirring frequently.

2 Meanwhile, add the turkey, potatoes, parsley and flour to the cooked bacon in the bowl. Stir and toss gently, then fold in the diced beetroot.

3 Add half the remaining butter to the frying pan, then the turkey vegetable mixture. Stir, then spread the mixture to evenly cover the bottom of the frying pan. Cook for 15 minutes, or until the underside is crisp and brown, pressing the hash firmly into a cake with a spatula. Remove from the heat.

4 Invert a large plate over the frying pan and, holding the plate and frying pan together with an oven glove, turn the hash out onto the plate. Heat the remaining butter in the pan, slide the hash back into the pan and cook for 4 minutes, or until crisp and brown on the other side. Invert onto the plate again and serve immediately with a green salad.

Ingredients   SERVES 4–6

2 tbsp vegetable oil
50 g/2 oz butter
4 slices streaky bacon, diced or sliced
1 medium onion, peeled and finely
  chopped
450 g/1 lb cooked turkey, diced
450 g/1 lb cooked potatoes,
  finely chopped
2–3 tbsp freshly chopped parsley
2 tbsp plain flour
250 g/9 oz cooked medium
  beetroot, diced
green salad, to serve

Tasty Tip

A hash is usually made just with potatoes, but here they are combined with ruby red beetroot, which adds vibrant colour and a sweet earthy flavour to the dish. Make sure that you buy plainly cooked beetroot rather than the type preserved in vinegar.

Aromatic Duck Burgers on Potato Pancakes

1 Peel off the thick layer of fat from the duck breasts and cut into small pieces. Put the fat in a small dry saucepan and set over a low heat for 10–15 minutes, or until the fat runs clear and the crackling goes crisp; reserve. Cut the duck meat into pieces and blend in a food processor until coarsely chopped. Spoon into a bowl and add the hoisin sauce, garlic, half the spring onions, soy sauce and Chinese five-spice powder. Season to taste with salt and pepper and shape into 4 burgers. Cover and chill in the refrigerator for 1 hour.

2 To make the potato pancakes, grate the potatoes into a large bowl, squeeze out the water with your hands, then put on a clean tea towel and twist the ends to squeeze out any remaining water. Return the potato to the bowl, add the onion and egg and mix well. Add the flour, salt and pepper. Stir to blend.

3 Heat about 2 tablespoons of the clear duck fat in a large frying pan. Spoon the potato mixture into 2–4 pattie shapes and cook for 6 minutes, or until golden and crisp, turning once. Keep warm in the oven. Repeat with the remaining mixture, adding duck fat as needed. Preheat the grill and line the grill rack with foil. Brush the burgers with a little of the duck fat and grill for 6–8 minutes, or longer if wished, turning once. Arrange 1–2 potato pancakes on a plate and top with a burger. Spoon over a little hoisin sauce and garnish with the remaining spring onions and coriander.

Ingredients   SERVES 4

700 g/1¹/₂ lb boneless duck breasts
2 tbsp hoisin sauce
1 garlic clove, peeled and finely chopped
4 spring onions, trimmed and finely chopped
2 tbsp Japanese soy sauce
¹/₂ tsp Chinese five-spice powder
salt and freshly ground black pepper
freshly chopped coriander, to garnish
extra hoisin sauce, to serve

For the potato pancakes:

450 g/1 lb floury potatoes
1 small onion, peeled and grated
1 small egg, beaten
1 heaped tbsp plain flour

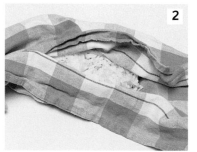

Vegetables

Potatoes provide a feast in their own right if you know what to do with them! Creamy Vegetable Korma and Spinach Dahl will stop you reaching for the takeaway menu, and our Roasted Mixed Vegetables with Garlic and Herb Sauce is wonderful on its own or as a side dish. Layered Cheese & Herb Potato Cake is lovely cold and sliced in a lunchbox, and Chargrilled Vegetable & Goats' Cheese Pizza is a great weekend supper.

Thai-style Cauliflower & Potato Curry

1 Bring a saucepan of lightly salted water to the boil, add the potatoes and cook for 15 minutes, or until just tender. Drain and leave to cool. Boil the cauliflower for 2 minutes, then drain and refresh under cold running water. Drain again and reserve.

2 Meanwhile, blend the garlic, onion, ground almonds and spices with 2 tablespoons of the oil and salt and pepper to taste in a food processor until a smooth paste is formed. Heat a wok, add the remaining oil and, when hot, add the spice paste and cook for 3–4 minutes, stirring continuously.

3 Dissolve the creamed coconut in 6 tablespoons of boiling water and add to the wok. Pour in the stock, cook for 2–3 minutes, then stir in the cooked potatoes and cauliflower.

4 Stir in the mango chutney and heat through for 3–4 minutes, or until piping hot. Tip into a warmed serving dish, garnish with sprigs of fresh coriander and serve immediately with freshly cooked rice.

Ingredients
SERVES 4

450 g/1 lb new potatoes, peeled
   and halved or quartered
350 g/12 oz cauliflower florets
3 garlic cloves, peeled and crushed
1 onion, peeled and finely chopped
40 g/1½ oz ground almonds
1 tsp ground coriander
½ tsp ground cumin
½ tsp turmeric
3 tbsp groundnut oil
salt and freshly ground black pepper
50 g/2 oz creamed coconut, broken
   into small pieces
200 ml/7 fl oz vegetable stock
1 tbsp mango chutney
sprigs of fresh coriander, to garnish
freshly cooked long-grain rice, to serve

Helpful Hint
Mildly flavoured vegetables absorb the taste and colour of spices in this dish. Take care not to overcook the cauliflower; it should be only just tender for this dish. Broccoli florets would make a good alternative.

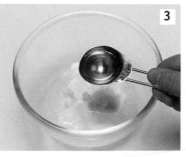

Vegetable Kofta Curry

1 Bring a saucepan of lightly salted water to the boil. Add the potatoes, carrots and parsnips. Cover and simmer for 12–15 minutes, or until the vegetables are tender. Drain the vegetables and mash until very smooth. Stir the egg into the vegetable purée, then add the flour and mix to make a stiff batter and reserve.

2 Heat 2 tablespoons of the oil in a wok and gently cook the onions for 10 minutes. Add the garlic and ginger and cook for a further 2–3 minutes, or until very soft and just beginning to colour.

3 Sprinkle the garam masala over the onions and stir in. Add the tomato paste and stock. Bring to the boil, cover and simmer gently for 15 minutes.

4 Meanwhile, heat the remaining oil in a wok or frying pan. Drop in tablespoons of vegetable batter, 4 or 5 at a time, and fry, turning often, for 3-4 minutes until brown and crisp. Remove with a slotted spoon and drain on absorbent kitchen paper. Keep warm in a low oven while cooking the rest.

5 Stir the yogurt and coriander into the onion sauce. Slowly heat to boiling point and season to taste with salt and pepper. Divide the koftas between warmed serving plates and spoon over the sauce. Serve immediately.

Ingredients   SERVES 6

350 g/12 oz potatoes, peeled and diced
225 g/8 oz carrots, peeled and roughly chopped
225 g/8 oz parsnips, peeled and roughly chopped
1 medium egg, lightly beaten
75 g/3 oz plain flour, sifted
8 tbsp sunflower oil
2 onions, peeled and sliced
2 garlic cloves, peeled and crushed
2.5 cm/1 inch piece fresh root ginger, peeled and grated
2 tbsp garam masala
2 tbsp tomato paste
300 ml/$\frac{1}{2}$ pint vegetable stock
250 ml/9 fl oz Greek-style yogurt
3 tbsp freshly chopped coriander
salt and freshly ground black pepper

Food Fact

Greek yogurt is made by straining the excess watery liquid from ordinary yogurt, making it thicker and higher in fat than natural yogurt.

Vegetable Frittata

1 Preheat the grill just before cooking. Lightly beat the eggs with the parsley, tarragon and half the cheese. Season to taste with black pepper and reserve. (Salt is not needed as the pecorino is very salty.)

2 Bring a large saucepan of lightly salted water to the boil. Add the new potatoes and cook for 8 minutes. Add the carrots and cook for 4 minutes, then add the broccoli florets and the courgettes and cook for a further 3–4 minutes, or until all the vegetables are barely tender. Drain well.

3 Heat the oil in a 20.5 cm/8 inch heavy-based frying pan. Add the spring onions and cook for 3–4 minutes, or until softened. Add all the vegetables and cook for a few seconds, then pour in the beaten egg mixture.

4 Stir gently for a minute, then cook for a further 1–2 minutes, or until the bottom of the frittata is set and golden brown.

5 Place the pan under a hot grill for 1 minute, or until almost set and just beginning to brown. Sprinkle with the remaining cheese and grill for a further 1 minute, or until it is lightly browned.

6 Loosen the edges and slide out of the pan. Cut into wedges and serve hot or warm with a mixed green salad and crusty Italian bread.

Ingredients SERVES 2

6 medium eggs
2 tbsp freshly chopped parsley
1 tbsp freshly chopped tarragon
25 g/1 oz pecorino or Parmesan
   cheese, finely grated
freshly ground black pepper
175 g/6 oz tiny new potatoes
2 small carrots, peeled and sliced
125 g/4 oz broccoli, cut into small florets
1 courgette, about 125 g/4 oz, sliced
2 tbsp olive oil
4 spring onions, trimmed and
   thinly sliced

To serve:
mixed green salad
crusty Italian bread

Food Fact
A frittata is a heavy omelette, usually with a vegetable, meat or cheese filling that is cooked slowly and often finished in the oven or under the grill. It is closer to a Spanish tortilla than to a classic French omelette.

Vegetable Biryani

1. Preheat the oven to 200°C/400°F/Gas Mark 6. Put 1 tablespoon of the vegetable oil in a large bowl with the onions and toss to coat. Lightly brush or spray a nonstick baking sheet with a little more oil. Spread half the onions on the baking sheet and cook at the top of the preheated oven for 25–30 minutes, stirring regularly, until golden and crisp. Remove from the oven and reserve for the garnish.

2. Meanwhile, heat a large flameproof casserole over a medium heat and add the remaining oil and onions. Cook for 5–7 minutes until softened and starting to brown. Add a little water if they start to stick. Add the garlic and ginger and cook for another minute, then add the carrot, parsnip and sweet potato. Cook the vegetables for a further 5 minutes. Add the curry paste and stir for a minute until everything is coated, then stir in the rice and tomatoes. After 2 minutes, add the stock and stir well. Bring to the boil, cover and simmer over a very gentle heat for about 10 minutes.

3. Add the cauliflower and peas and cook for 8–10 minutes, or until the rice is tender. Season to taste with salt and pepper. Serve garnished with the crispy onions, cashew nuts, raisins and coriander.

Ingredients   SERVES 4

2 tbsp vegetable oil, plus a little extra
    for brushing
2 large onions, peeled and thinly sliced
    lengthways
2 garlic cloves, peeled and finely
    chopped
2.5 cm/1 inch piece fresh root ginger,
    peeled and finely grated
1 small carrot, peeled and cut into sticks
1 small parsnip, peeled and diced
1 small sweet potato, peeled and diced
1 tbsp medium curry paste
225 g/8 oz basmati rice
4 ripe tomatoes, peeled, deseeded
    and diced
600 ml/1 pint vegetable stock
175 g/6 oz cauliflower (such as
    Romanesco) florets
50 g/2 oz peas, thawed if frozen
salt and freshly ground black pepper

To garnish:
roasted cashew nuts
raisins
fresh coriander leaves

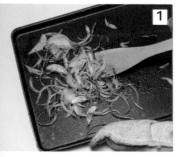

Roasted Mixed Vegetables with Garlic & Herb Sauce

1   Preheat the oven to 220°C/425°F/Gas Mark 7. Cut the garlic in half horizontally. Put into a large roasting tin with all the vegetables and herbs.

2   Add the oil, season well with salt and pepper and toss together to coat lightly in the oil.

3   Cover with foil and roast in the preheated oven for 50 minutes. Remove the foil and cook for a further 30 minutes until all the vegetables are tender and slightly charred.

4   Remove the tin from the oven and allow to cool.

5   In a small saucepan, melt the low-fat soft cheese together with the milk and lemon zest.

6   Remove the garlic from the roasting tin and squeeze the flesh into a bowl. Mash thoroughly, then add to the sauce. Heat through gently. Pour some sauce into small ramekins and garnish with sprigs of thyme. Season the vegetables to taste and serve immediately with dipping sauce.

Ingredients   SERVES 4

1 large garlic bulb
1 large onion, peeled and cut
    into wedges
4 small carrots, peeled and quartered
4 small parsnips, peeled
6 small potatoes, scrubbed and halved
1 fennel bulb, thickly sliced
4 sprigs of fresh rosemary
4 sprigs of fresh thyme
2 tbsp olive oil
salt and freshly ground black pepper
200 g/7 oz low-fat soft cheese with
    herbs and garlic
4 tbsp milk
zest of ½ lemon
sprigs of thyme, to garnish

Tasty Tip

This dish can also be served as an accompaniment to any grilled or roasted fish, seafood or chicken dish. Following the Mediterranean theme, marinade or drizzle the fish with a little olive oil, lemon juice and mixed herbs.

Mediterranean Feast

1 Cut the lettuce into 4 and remove the hard core. Tear into bite-size pieces and arrange on a large serving platter or 4 individual plates.

2 Cook the French beans in boiling salted water for 8 minutes and the potatoes for 10 minutes, or until tender. Drain and rinse in cold water until cool, then cut both the beans and potatoes in half with a sharp knife.

3 Boil the eggs for 10 minutes, then rinse thoroughly under a cold running tap until cool. Remove the shells under water and cut each egg into 4.

4 Remove the seeds from the pepper and cut into thin strips and finely chop the onion.

5 Arrange the beans, potatoes, eggs, peppers and onion on top of the lettuce. Add the tuna, cheese and tomatoes. Sprinkle over the olives and garnish with the basil.

6 To make the vinaigrette, place all the ingredients in a screw-topped jar and shake vigorously until everything is mixed thoroughly. Spoon 4 tablespoons over the top of the prepared salad and serve the remainder separately.

Ingredients　　　SERVES 4

1 small iceberg lettuce
225 g/8 oz French beans
225 g/8 oz baby new potatoes, scrubbed
4 medium eggs
1 green pepper
1 medium onion, peeled
200 g can tuna in brine, drained and flaked into small pieces
50 g/2 oz low-fat hard cheese, such as Edam, cut into small cubes
8 ripe but firm cherry tomatoes, quartered
50 g/2 oz black pitted olives, halved
freshly chopped basil, to garnish

For the lime vinaigrette:

3 tbsp light olive oil
2 tbsp white wine vinegar
4 tbsp lime juice
grated rind of 1 lime
1 tsp Dijon mustard
1-2 tsp caster sugar
salt and freshly ground black pepper

Beetroot & Potato Medley

1 Preheat the oven to 180°C/350°F/Gas Mark 4. Scrub the beetroot thoroughly and place on a baking tray.

2 Brush the beetroot with a little oil and cook for 1½ hours, or until a skewer is easily insertable into the beetroot. Allow to cool a little, then remove the skins.

3 Cook the potatoes in boiling water for about 10 minutes. Rinse in cold water and drain. Reserve the potatoes until cool. Dice evenly.

4 Cut the cucumber into cubes and place in a mixing bowl. Chop the beetroot into small cubes and add to the bowl with the reserved potatoes. Gently mix the vegetables together.

5 Mix together the vinegar and yogurt and season to taste with a little salt and pepper. Pour over the vegetables and combine gently.

6 Arrange on a bed of salad leaves garnished with the snipped chives and serve.

Ingredients SERVES 4

350 g/12 oz raw baby beetroot
½ tsp sunflower oil
225 g/8 oz new potatoes
½ cucumber, peeled
3 tbsp white wine vinegar
150 ml/5 fl oz low-fat natural yogurt
salt and freshly ground black pepper
fresh salad leaves
1 tbsp freshly snipped chives, to garnish

Helpful Hint

Beetroot can also be cooked in the microwave. Place in a microwaveable bowl. Add sufficient water to come halfway up the sides of the bowl. Cover and cook for 10–15 minutes on high. Leave for 5 minutes before uncovering. Cook before peeling.

Food Fact

Like other fruits and vegetables which are red in colour, beetroot has particularly high levels of antioxidants which are essential to the body to fight disease.

Leek & Potato Tart

1 Preheat the oven to 200°C/400°F/Gas Mark 6, about 15 minutes before baking. Sift the flour and salt into a bowl. Rub in the butter until the mixture resembles breadcrumbs. Stir in the nuts. Mix together the egg yolk and 3 tablespoons of cold water. Sprinkle over the dry ingredients. Mix to form a dough.

2 Knead on a lightly floured surface for a few seconds, then wrap in clingfilm and chill in the refrigerator for 20 minutes. Roll out and use to line a 20.5 cm/8 inch spring-form tin or very deep flan tin. Chill for a further 30 minutes.

3 Cook the leeks in the butter over a high heat for 2–3 minutes, stirring constantly. Lower the heat, cover and cook for 25 minutes until soft, stirring occasionally. Remove the leeks from the heat.

4 Cook the potatoes in boiling salted water for 15 minutes, or until almost tender. Drain and slice thickly. Add to the leeks. Stir the soured cream into the leeks and potatoes, followed by the eggs, cheese, nutmeg and salt and pepper. Pour into the pastry case and bake on the middle shelf in the preheated oven for 20 minutes.

5 Reduce the oven temperature to 190°C/375°F/Gas Mark 5 and cook for a further 30–35 minutes, or until the filling is set. Garnish with chives and serve immediately.

Ingredients   SERVES 6

225 g/8 oz plain flour
pinch of salt
150 g/5 oz butter, cubed
50 g/2 oz walnuts, very finely chopped
1 large egg yolk

For the filling:

450 g/1 lb leeks, trimmed and
   thinly sliced
40 g/1½ oz butter
450 g/1 lb large new potatoes,
   scrubbed
300 ml/½ pint soured cream
3 medium eggs, lightly beaten
175 g/6 oz Gruyère cheese, grated
freshly grated nutmeg
salt and freshly ground black pepper
fresh chives, to garnish

Tasty Tip

To ring the changes, flavour the pastry with different nuts, such as hazelnuts or almonds, or replace the nuts with 3 tablespoons of freshly chopped mixed herbs.

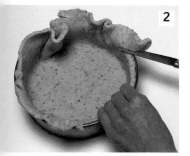

Potato Gnocchi with Pesto Sauce

1 Cook the potatoes in their skins in boiling water for 20 minutes, or until tender. Drain and peel. While still warm, push the potatoes through a fine sieve into a bowl. Stir in the butter, egg, 175 g/6 oz of the flour, and the salt and pepper.

2 Sift the remaining flour onto a board or work surface add the potato mixture. Gently knead in enough flour until a soft, slightly sticky dough is formed.

3 With floured hands, break off portions of the dough and roll into 2.5 cm/1 inch thick ropes. Cut into 2 cm/³/₄ inch lengths. Lightly press each piece against the inner prongs of a fork. Put on a tray, cover with a floured tea towel and chill in the refrigerator for about 30 minutes.

4 To make the pesto sauce, put the basil, garlic, pine nuts and oil in a processor and blend until smooth and creamy. Turn into a bowl and stir in the Parmesan cheese. Season to taste.

5 Cooking in several batches, drop the gnocchi into a saucepan of barely simmering salted water. Cook for 3–4 minutes, or until they float to the surface. Remove with a slotted spoon and keep warm in a covered oiled baking dish in a low oven. When all the gnocchi are cooked, add them to the pesto sauce and toss gently to coat. Serve immediately, scattered with the Parmesan cheese and accompanied by a rocket salad.

Ingredients   SERVES 6
900 g/2 lb floury potatoes
40 g/1¹/₂ oz butter
1 medium egg, beaten
225 g/8 oz plain flour
1 tsp salt
freshly ground black pepper
25 g/1 oz Parmesan cheese, shaved
rocket salad, to serve

For the pesto sauce:
50 g/2 oz fresh basil leaves
1 large garlic clove, peeled
2 tbsp pine nuts
125 ml/4 fl oz olive oil
40 g/1¹/₂ oz Parmesan cheese, grated

Helpful Hint
Use a vegetable peeler to pare the Parmesan cheese into decorative thin curls.

Vegetarian Cassoulet

1 Preheat the oven to 180°C/350°F/Gas Mark 4, 10 minutes before required. Drain the beans, rinse under cold running water and put in a saucepan. Peel 1 of the onions and add to the beans with the bay leaf. Pour in the water.

2 Bring to a rapid boil and cook for 10 minutes, then turn down the heat, cover and simmer for 50 minutes, or until the beans are almost tender. Drain the beans, reserving the liquor, but discarding the onion and bay leaf.

3 Cook the potatoes in a saucepan of lightly salted boiling water for 6–7 minutes until almost tender when tested with the point of a knife. Drain and reserve.

4 Peel and chop the remaining onion. Heat the oil in a frying pan and cook the onion with the garlic and leeks for 10 minutes until softened. Stir in the tomatoes, sugar, thyme and parsley. Stir in the beans with 300 ml/¹/₂ pint of the reserved liquor and season to taste. Simmer, uncovered, for 5 minutes.

5 Layer the potato slices, courgettes and ladlefuls of the bean mixture in a large flameproof casserole. To make the topping, mix together the breadcrumbs and cheese and sprinkle over the top. Bake in the preheated oven for 40 minutes, or until the vegetables are cooked through and the topping is golden brown and crisp. Serve immediately.

Ingredients   SERVES 4

225 g/8 oz dried haricot beans,
   soaked overnight
2 medium onions
1 bay leaf
1.4 litres/2¹/₂ pints cold water
550 g/1¹/₄ lb large potatoes, peeled
   and cut into 1 cm/¹/₂ inch slices
salt and freshly ground black pepper
5 tsp olive oil
1 large garlic clove, peeled
   and crushed
2 leeks, trimmed and sliced
200 g can chopped tomatoes
1 tsp dark muscovado sugar
1 tbsp freshly chopped thyme
2 tbsp freshly chopped parsley
3 courgettes, trimmed and sliced

For the topping:

50 g/2 oz fresh white breadcrumbs
25 g/1 oz Cheddar cheese,
   finely grated

Sweet Potato Cakes with Mango & Tomato Salsa

1 Steam or cook the sweet potatoes in lightly salted boiling water for 15–20 minutes, until tender. Drain well, then mash until smooth.

2 Melt the butter in a saucepan. Add the onion and garlic and cook gently for 10 minutes until soft. Add to the mashed sweet potato and season with the nutmeg, salt and pepper. Stir together until mixed thoroughly. Leave to cool.

3 Shape the mixture into 4 oval potato cakes, about 2.5 cm/1 inch thick. Dip first in the beaten egg, allowing the excess to fall back into the bowl, then coat in the polenta. Refrigerate for at least 30 minutes.

4 Meanwhile, mix together all the ingredients for the salsa. Spoon into a serving bowl, cover with clingfilm and leave at room temperature to allow the flavours to develop.

5 Heat the oil in a frying pan and cook the potato cakes for 4–5 minutes on each side. Serve with the salsa and salad leaves.

Ingredients SERVES 4

700 g/1½ lb sweet potatoes, peeled and cut into large chunks
salt and freshly ground black pepper
25 g/1 oz butter
1 onion, peeled and chopped
1 garlic clove, peeled and crushed
pinch of freshly grated nutmeg
1 medium egg, beaten
50 g/2 oz quick-cook polenta
2 tbsp sunflower oil

For the salsa:

1 ripe mango, peeled, stoned and diced
6 cherry tomatoes, cut into wedges
4 spring onions, trimmed and thinly sliced
1 red chilli, deseeded and finely chopped
finely grated rind and juice of ½ lime
2 tbsp freshly chopped mint
1 tsp clear honey
salad leaves, to serve

Cheese & Onion Oat Pie

1 Preheat the oven to 180°C/350°F/Gas Mark 4. Heat the tablespoon of oil and half the butter in a saucepan until melted. Add the onions and garlic and cook gently for 10 minutes, or until soft. Remove from the heat and tip into a large bowl.

2 Spread the oats out on a baking sheet and toast in the hot oven for 12 minutes. Leave to cool, then add to the onions with the cheese, eggs and parsley. Season to taste with salt and pepper and mix well.

3 Line the base of a 20.5 cm/8 inch round sandwich tin with greaseproof paper and oil well. Thinly slice the potato and arrange the slices on the base, overlapping them slightly.

4 Spoon the cheese and oat mixture on top of the potato, spreading evenly with the back of a spoon. Cover with foil and bake for 30 minutes.

5 Invert the pie onto a baking sheet so that the potatoes are on top. Carefully remove the tin and lining paper.

6 Preheat the grill to medium. Melt the remaining butter and carefully brush over the potato topping. Cook under the preheated grill for 5–6 minutes until the potatoes are lightly browned. Cut into wedges and serve.

Ingredients   SERVES 4

1 tbsp sunflower oil, plus 1 tsp
  for oiling
25 g/1 oz butter
2 medium onions, peeled and sliced
1 garlic clove, peeled and crushed
150 g/5 oz porridge oats
125 g/4 oz mature Cheddar cheese,
  grated
2 medium eggs, lightly beaten
2 tbsp freshly chopped parsley
salt and freshly ground black pepper
275 g/10 oz baking potato, peeled

Tasty Tip

To add flavour to this dish, cook the onions very slowly until soft and just beginning to colour and caramelise – either white or red onions can be used. For a crunchier texture, add 50 g/2 oz chopped hazelnuts instead of 50 g/2 oz of the oats, adding them to the baking sheet of oats for the last 5 minutes of cooking time, in step 2.

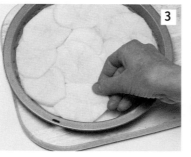

Chargrilled Vegetable & Goats' Cheese Pizza

1 Preheat the oven to 220°C/425°F/Gas Mark 7, 15 minutes before baking. Put a baking sheet in the oven to heat up. Cook the potato in lightly salted boiling water until tender. Peel and mash with the olive oil until smooth.

2 Sift the flour and salt into a bowl. Stir in the yeast. Add the mashed potato and 150 ml/¼ pint warm water and mix to a soft dough. Knead for 5–6 minutes until smooth. Put the dough in a bowl, cover with clingfilm and leave to rise in a warm place for 30 minutes.

3 To make the topping, arrange the aubergine, courgettes, pepper and onion, skin-side up, on a grill rack and brush with 4 tablespoons of the oil. Grill for 4–5 minutes. Turn the vegetables and brush with the remaining oil. Grill for 3–4 minutes. Cool, skin and slice the pepper. Put all of the vegetables in a bowl, add the halved new potatoes and toss gently together. Set aside.

4 Briefly re-knead the dough, then roll out to a 30.5–35.5 cm/12–14 inch round, according to preferred thickness. Mix the tomatoes and oregano together and spread over the pizza base. Scatter over the mozzarella cheese. Put the pizza on the preheated baking sheet and bake for 8 minutes, then arrange the vegetables and goats' cheese on top and bake for 8–10 minutes. Serve.

Ingredients SERVES 4

125 g/4 oz baking potato
1 tbsp olive oil
225 g/8 oz strong white flour
½ tsp salt
1 tsp easy-blend dried yeast

For the topping:

1 medium aubergine, thinly sliced
2 small courgettes, trimmed and
    sliced lengthways
1 yellow pepper, quartered and
    deseeded
1 red onion, peeled and sliced into
    very thin wedges
5 tbsp olive oil
175 g/6 oz cooked new potatoes,
    halved
400 g can chopped tomatoes,
    drained
2 tsp freshly chopped oregano
125 g/4 oz mozzarella cheese, cut
    into small cubes
125 g/4 oz goats' cheese, crumbled

Chunky Vegetable & Fennel Goulash with Dumplings

1 Cut the fennel bulbs in half widthways. Thickly slice the stalks and cut the bulbs into 8 wedges. Heat the oil in a large saucepan or flameproof casserole. Add the onion and fennel and cook gently for 10 minutes until soft. Stir in the paprika and flour.

2 Remove from the heat and gradually stir in the stock. Add the chopped tomatoes, potatoes and mushrooms. Season to taste with salt and pepper. Bring to the boil, reduce the heat and simmer for 20 minutes.

3 Meanwhile, make the dumplings. Heat the oil in a frying pan and gently cook the onion for 10 minutes until soft. Leave to cool for a few minutes.

4 In a bowl, beat the egg and milk together, then add the onion, parsley and breadcrumbs and season to taste. With damp hands, form the breadcrumb mixture into 12 round dumplings, each about the size of a walnut.

5 Arrange the dumplings on top of the goulash. Cover and cook for a further 15 minutes, until the dumplings are cooked and the vegetables are tender. Serve immediately.

Ingredients SERVES 4

2 fennel bulbs, weighing about 450 g/1 lb
2 tbsp sunflower oil
1 large onion, peeled and sliced
1$^1/_2$ tbsp paprika
1 tbsp plain flour
300 ml/$^1/_2$ pint vegetable stock
400 g can chopped tomatoes
450 g/1 lb potatoes, peeled and cut into 2.5 cm/1 inch chunks
125 g/4 oz small button mushrooms
salt and freshly ground black pepper

For the dumplings:

1 tbsp sunflower oil
1 small onion, peeled and finely chopped
1 medium egg
3 tbsp milk
3 tbsp freshly chopped parsley
125 g/4 oz fresh white breadcrumbs

Creamy Vegetable Korma

1 Heat the ghee or oil in a large saucepan. Add the onion and cook for 5 minutes. Stir in the garlic and ginger and cook for a further 5 minutes, or until soft and just beginning to colour.

2 Stir in the cardamom, ground coriander, cumin and turmeric. Continue cooking over a low heat for 1 minute, stirring.

3 Stir in the lemon rind and juice and almonds. Blend in the vegetable stock. Slowly bring to the boil, stirring occasionally.

4 Add the potatoes and vegetables. Bring back to the boil, then reduce the heat, cover and simmer for 35–40 minutes, or until the vegetables are just tender. Check after 25 minutes and add a little more stock if needed.

5 Slowly stir in the cream and chopped coriander. Season to taste with salt and pepper. Cook very gently until heated through, but do not boil. Serve immediately with naan bread.

Ingredients   SERVES 4–6

2 tbsp ghee or vegetable oil
1 large onion, peeled and chopped
2 garlic cloves, peeled and crushed
2.5 cm/1 inch piece root ginger, peeled and grated
4 cardamom pods
2 tsp ground coriander
1 tsp ground cumin
1 tsp ground turmeric
finely grated rind and juice of $\frac{1}{2}$ lemon
50 g/2 oz ground almonds
400 ml/14 fl oz vegetable stock
450 g/1 lb potatoes, peeled and diced
450 g/1 lb mixed vegetables, such as cauliflower, carrots and turnip, cut into chunks
150 ml/$\frac{1}{4}$ pint double cream
3 tbsp freshly chopped coriander
salt and freshly ground black pepper
naan bread, to serve

Indonesian Salad with Peanut Dressing

1 Cook the potatoes in a saucepan of boiling salted water for 15–20 minutes until tender. Remove with a slotted spoon and thickly slice into a large bowl. Keep the saucepan of water boiling.

2 Add the carrot, French beans and cauliflower to the water, return to the boil and cook for 2 minutes, or until just tender. Drain and refresh under cold running water, then drain well. Add to the potatoes with the cucumber and bean sprouts.

3 To make the dressing, gently heat the sesame oil in a small saucepan. Add the garlic and chilli and cook for a few seconds, then remove from the heat. Stir in the peanut butter.

4 Stir in the stock, a little at a time. Add the remaining ingredients and mix together to make a thick, creamy dressing.

5 Divide the vegetables between 4 plates and arrange the eggs on top. Drizzle the dressing over the salad and serve immediately.

Ingredients   SERVES 4

225 g/8 oz new potatoes, scrubbed
1 large carrot, peeled and cut into matchsticks
125 g/4 oz French beans, trimmed
225 g/8 oz tiny cauliflower florets
125 g/4 oz cucumber, cut into matchsticks
75 g/3 oz fresh bean sprouts
3 medium eggs, hard-boiled and quartered

For the peanut dressing:

2 tbsp sesame oil
1 garlic clove, peeled and crushed
1 red chilli, deseeded and finely chopped
150 g/5 oz crunchy peanut butter
6 tbsp hot vegetable stock
2 tsp soft light brown sugar
2 tsp dark soy sauce
1 tbsp lime juice

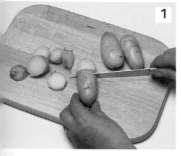

Layered Cheese & Herb Potato Cake

1 Preheat the oven to 180°C/350°F/Gas Mark 4. Lightly oil and line the base of a 20.5 cm/8 inch round cake tin with lightly oiled greaseproof paper or baking parchment. Peel and thinly slice the potatoes and reserve. Stir the chives, parsley, cheese and egg yolks together in a small bowl and reserve. Mix the paprika into the breadcrumbs.

2 Sprinkle the almonds over the base of the lined tin. Cover with half the potatoes, arranging them in layers, then sprinkle with the paprika breadcrumb mixture and season to taste with salt and pepper.

3 Spoon the cheese and herb mixture over the breadcrumbs with a little more seasoning, then arrange the remaining potatoes on top. Drizzle over the melted butter and press the surface down firmly.

4 Bake in the preheated oven for 1¼ hours, or until golden and cooked through. Let the tin stand for 10 minutes before carefully turning out and serving in thick wedges. Serve immediately with salad or freshly cooked vegetables.

Ingredients   SERVES 4

900 g/2 lb waxy potatoes
3 tbsp freshly snipped chives
2 tbsp freshly chopped parsley
225 g/8 oz mature Cheddar cheese
2 large egg yolks
1 tsp paprika
125 g/4 oz fresh white breadcrumbs
50 g/2 oz almonds, toasted and
   roughly chopped
50 g/2 oz butter, melted
salt and freshly ground black pepper
mixed salad or steamed vegetables,
   to serve

Handy Hint

Check that the potatoes are tender all the way through by pushing a thin skewer through the centre. If the potatoes are still a little hard and the top is already brown enough, loosely cover with a piece of foil and continue cooking until done.

Baby Roast Potato Salad

1 Preheat the oven to 200°C/400°F/Gas Mark 6. Trim the shallots, but leave the skins on. Put in a saucepan of lightly salted boiling water with the potatoes and cook for 5 minutes; drain. Separate the shallots and plunge them into cold water for 1 minute.

2 Put the oil in a baking sheet lined with foil or a roasting tin and heat for a few minutes. Peel the skins off the shallots – they should now come away easily. Add to the baking sheet or roasting tin with the potatoes and toss in the oil to coat. Sprinkle with a little sea salt. Roast the potatoes and shallots in the preheated oven for 10 minutes.

3 Meanwhile, trim the courgettes, halve lengthways and cut into 5 cm/2 inch chunks. Add to the baking sheet or roasting tin, toss to mix and cook for 5 minutes.

4 Pierce the tomato skins with a sharp knife. Add to the sheet or tin with the rosemary and cook for a further 5 minutes, or until all the vegetables are tender. Remove the rosemary and discard. Grind a little black pepper over the vegetables.

5 Spoon into a wide serving bowl. Mix together the soured cream and chives and drizzle over the vegetables just before serving.

Ingredients   SERVES 4

350 g/12 oz small shallots
sea salt and freshly ground black pepper
900 g/2 lb small even-sized new potatoes
2 tbsp olive oil
2 medium courgettes
2 sprigs of fresh rosemary
175 g/6 oz cherry tomatoes
150 ml/¼ pint soured cream
2 tbsp freshly snipped chives
¼ tsp paprika

Tasty Tip

For a more substantial salad or to serve 6 rather than 4 people, add 225 g/8 oz baby aubergines, cut in half lengthways and cook with the potatoes and shallots, along with an extra 1 tablespoon of olive oil. If you prefer, crème fraîche or Greek-style yogurt may be used instead of the soured cream.

Curried Potatoes with Spinach

1 Cut the potatoes into small cubes and reserve. Dry-fry the cumin seeds in a saucepan for 30 seconds, then add the oil and potatoes and cook for 3–5 minutes, stirring, or until the potatoes are beginning to turn golden.

2 Add the onion, garlic and chilli and continue to cook for 2–3 minutes, or until the onion is beginning to soften. Sprinkle in the ground coriander and turmeric and cook for a further 2 minutes.

3 Chop the tomatoes and stir into the pan. Cover and cook, stirring occasionally, for 10 minutes, or until the potatoes are tender. Stir in the spinach, water and seasoning, to taste, and cook for 2 minutes, or until the spinach has wilted, then serve.

Ingredients   SERVES 4–6

300 g/10 oz potatoes, peeled
1 tsp cumin seeds
2 tbsp vegetable oil
1 onion, peeled and chopped
2 garlic cloves, peeled and crushed
1 red chilli, deseeded and
    finely chopped
1 tsp ground coriander
$^1/_2$ tsp turmeric
4 tomatoes
450 g/1 lb fresh leaf spinach, lightly
    rinsed and chopped
50 ml/2 fl oz water
salt and freshly ground black pepper

Tasty Tip:
This is an ideal accompaniment for all curries as well as being a good snack for lunch or supper.

Mung Bean Curry

1 Break the coconut into small pieces and place in a food processor or liquidiser with one of the chillies and 3 tablespoons of water. Blend for 1 minute, then, with the motor still running, gradually pour in the remaining water to form a thin, smooth liquid. Reserve.

2 Place the mung beans, remaining chilli and turmeric in a saucepan and cover with water. Bring to the boil, then reduce the heat and simmer for 20 minutes. Cut the potatoes into small chunks and add to the saucepan together with the onion and French beans. Continue to cook for 8 minutes.

3 Pour in the coconut liquid and cook, stirring occasionally, for a further 10 minutes, or until the beans and vegetables are tender.

4 Meanwhile, heat the oil in a small frying pan, add the mustard seeds and the curry leaves and fry for 1 minute, or until the mustard seeds pop. Stir well, then stir into the curry. Serve.

Ingredients   SERVES 4–6

50 g/2 oz creamed coconut
2 red chillies, deseeded and
　finely chopped
250 ml/8 fl oz water
250 g/9 oz canned mung beans
$^1/_2$ tsp turmeric
225 g/8 oz potatoes, peeled
1 onion, peeled and cut into wedges
175 g/6 oz French beans, trimmed
　and chopped
2 tbsp vegetable oil
1 tsp brown mustard seeds
5–6 curry leaves

Helpful Hint

If you cannot find canned mung beans, then use dried ones. You will need to soak them overnight before cooking. After soaking, rinse, then boil rapidly for 10 minutes, before reducing the heat and simmering for about 20 minutes, or until tender.

Spinach Dhal

1   Rinse the lentils and place in a saucepan with the onions, potato, chilli, water and turmeric. Bring to the boil, then reduce the heat, cover and simmer for 15 minutes, or until the lentils are tender and most of the liquid has been absorbed.

2   Chop the spinach and add to the pan with the tomatoes and cook for a further 5 minutes, or until the spinach has wilted.

3   Heat the oil in a frying pan, add the mustard seeds and fry for 1 minute, or until they pop. Add the curry leaves, stir well, then stir into the dhal and serve.

Ingredients   SERVES 4–6

100 g/3½ oz split red lentils

2 onions, peeled and chopped

225 g/8 oz potato, peeled and cut into small chunks

1 green chilli, deseeded and chopped

150 ml/¼ pint water

1 tsp turmeric

175 g/6 oz fresh spinach

2 tomatoes, chopped

2 tbsp vegetable oil

1 tsp mustard seeds

few curry leaves

Helpful Hint

It is important that spices are stored correctly otherwise their flavour can be impaired. Unless you use a lot of spice, buy in small quantities and store in a cool dark place. If you have time, grind your own spice powders to give a greater and more flavourful aroma and taste.

Sweet Potato Curry

1 Heat the oil in a sauté pan or wok, add the chillies, ginger and spices and fry for 3 minutes, stirring frequently. Add the onions and garlic and continue to fry for a further 5 minutes, or until the onion has softened.

2 Add the sweet potatoes and stir until coated in the spices, then add the green pepper and chopped tomatoes.

3 Pour in the coconut milk. Bring to the boil, then reduce the heat, cover and simmer for 12–15 minutes, or until the vegetables are cooked. Stir in the spinach and heat for 3 minutes, or until wilted. Add the curry leaves, stir and serve.

Ingredients   SERVES 4–6

2 tbsp vegetable oil
2 green chillies, deseeded and chopped
5 cm/2 inch piece fresh root ginger, peeled and grated
$1/2$–1 tsp chilli powder
1 tsp turmeric
1 tsp ground cumin
1 tsp ground coriander
2 onions, peeled and cut into wedges
2–3 garlic cloves, peeled and crushed
450 g/1 lb sweet potatoes, peeled and cut into small chunks
1 large green pepper, deseeded and chopped
4 tomatoes, chopped
300 ml/$^1/_2$ pint coconut milk
225 g/8 oz fresh spinach leaves
few curry leaves

Helpful Hint

As curry leaves are not that easy to find, it is worth buying a good number, then wrapping them well in freezer wrap and freezing.

Mixed Vegetable Curry

1 Heat the oil in a large saucepan or wok, add the seeds and fry for 30 seconds, or until they pop.

2 Add the garlic, curry powder and onions and cook gently for 5 minutes, or until the onions have softened.

3 Add the remaining vegetables, except for the peas and tomatoes, to the pan. Add the water, bring to the boil, then reduce the heat, cover and simmer for 15 minutes.

4 Add the peas and tomatoes and continue to simmer for a further 5 minutes. Stir in the curry leaves, ground almonds and yogurt. Heat gently for 3 minutes, or until hot. Garnish with chopped coriander and serve.

Ingredients   SERVES 4–6

2 tbsp vegetable oil

1 tsp cumin seeds

1 tsp black mustard seeds

2–3 garlic cloves, peeled and chopped

1 tbsp hot curry powder

2 onions, peeled and cut into wedges

225 g/8 oz sweet potatoes, peeled and chopped

225 g/8 oz potatoes, peeled and chopped

175 g/6 oz carrots, peeled and chopped

175 g/6 oz cauliflower, cut into small florets

300 ml/½ pint water

100 g/3½ oz frozen peas

3 tomatoes, chopped

few fresh curry leaves, chopped

2 tbsp ground almonds

4 tbsp natural yogurt

1 tbsp freshly chopped coriander, to garnish

Tasty Tip

For more substance, add a drained and rinsed 400 g/14 oz can of chickpeas.

Vegetable & Coconut Stew

1 Heat the oil or ghee in a large saucepan, add the seeds, cinnamon stick, cloves, cardamom pods and chilli powder and fry for 30 seconds, or until the seeds pop.

2 Add the shallots, garlic, potatoes, squash and carrots and stir until the vegetables are coated in the flavoured oil. Add the water, bring to the boil, then reduce the heat, cover and simmer for 15 minutes.

3 Pour in the coconut milk and add the chopped beans and kidney beans. Stir well, then cook for a further 10 minutes. Sprinkle with the chopped spring onions and serve.

Ingredients   SERVES 4–6

2 tbsp vegetable oil or ghee
1 tsp cumin seeds
1 cinnamon stick, bruised
3 whole cloves
3 cardamom pods, bruised
$^1/_2$–1 tsp chilli powder
8 shallots, peeled and halved
2–3 garlic cloves, peeled and
    finely chopped
225 g/8 oz potatoes, peeled and
    cut into chunks
$^1/_2$ butternut squash, about 350 g/12
    oz in weight, peeled, deseeded and
    cut into chunks
225 g/8 oz carrots, peeled
    and chopped
200 ml/7 fl oz water
300 ml/$^1/_2$ pint coconut milk
225 g/8 oz French beans, trimmed and
    chopped
400 g/14 oz can red kidney beans,
    drained and rinsed
4–6 spring onions, trimmed and
    finely chopped

Index